Aspects of Tantra Yoga

Debabrata SenSharma

INDICA

Published in 2007 by
Indica Books
D 40/18 Godowlia
Varanasi - 221 001 (U.P.)
India
E-mail: indicabooks@satyam.net.in

ISBN: 81-86569-67-7

Printed in India by First Impression, India
011-22481754, 09811224048

Pañcamukhī Śiva, B.H.U. Viśvanāth Mandir, Vārāṇasī

Dedicated
with profound respects and gratitude
to the hallowed memory of
Mahāmahopādhyāya Dr. Gopināth Kavirāj
who initiated me in the study
of the mysteries of Tantra Yoga

Contents

Blessing . . 11
Abbreviations . . 12
Preface . . 13

Chapter I ***Tantra — its Meaning, Scope and Extent*** **17**

What is Tantra . . 17
Origin of the Tantras . . 19
Scope of the Tāntrika cult . . 22
Origin and development of the Tāntrika literature . 23
Division of the Tāntrika tradition . . 25
Śaiva Tāntrika literature . . 25
Śaiva Tāntrika schools . . 32
Śākta Tāntrika literature . . 34
Śākta Tāntrika schools . . 41

Chapter II ***Salient Features of the Language of the Tantras*** **52**

Chapter III ***The Supreme Reality in the Śaiva Tantras*** **59**

Parāsaṁvid as the Supreme Reality . . 60
Divine Śakti, her nature and role in the manifestation of the universe 61

Chapter IV ***Nature of Man in the Śaiva Śākta Tantras*** **70**

Man, a self-manifested form of the Supreme Reality . 70
Defilements (*malas*), the cause for the manifestation of limited beings 71
Āṇavamala . . 71
Māyīyamala . . 75
Kārmamala . . 77

Chapter V ***Spiritual Discipline (Sādhana Kriyā) — and the Supreme Goal*** **80**

Evolution (*aroha*) — involuntary and as a result of spiritual discipline 80
Steps leading to the attainment of the Supreme Goal . 82

Chapter VI ***Śaktipāta and Guru*** **89**

Śaktipāta and its role in spiritual discipline . 89
Guru (divine teacher) and his kinds . 96

Chapter VII ***Dīkṣā (Initiation)*** **103**

Dīkṣā, its meaning and role in spiritual discipline . 103
Kinds of *dīkṣā* . 104

Chapter VIII ***Nature and Role of Mantra in Spiritual Practices in the Tāntrika Tradition*** **118**

Meaning of the term '*mantra*' . 119
Kinds of *mantra* and their use in *sādhanakriyā* . 120

Chapter IX ***Modes of Spiritual Discipline (Sādhanakriyā) in the Tāntrika Tradition*** **127**

Upāyas (modes of spiritual discipline) . . 129
Nature of *prāṇa* and its use in *sādhanā* (*prāṇoccāra*) . 131
Treatment of *prāṇa* in some select ancient Upaniṣads . 132
Nature of *prāṇa* in some schools of Indian Philosophy . 134
Nature of *prāṇa* and its place in *sādhanakriyā* in the Āgamic tradition 136

Chapter X ***The Supreme Goal, Śivatva*** **147**

Select Bibliography . . 151
Glossary . . 155
Index . . 158

Blessing

Nothing gives a teacher more joy and satisfaction than to find his student surpassing him in glory and attainment. This actually happened in the case of Professor Dr. Debabrata Sen Sharma, who is now associated with the Research Department of the Ramakrishna Mission Institute of Culture, Kolkata, supervising and helping in the execution of various research projects on Indology taken up there.

Sen Sharma, at that time, more than a half century back, was an earnest student in Sanskrit at the Banaras Hindu University (BHU) and I had the privilege to teach him for a couple of years or so. He was extremely fortunate to have contacted my most revered teacher, Mahamahopadhyaya Dr. Gopinath Kaviraj, who took him under his loving care to initiate him into the studies of Kashmir Shaivism, which was at that time almost an unknown branch of study, unique in its outlook and synthetic approach.

Thereafter, Sen Sharma never looked back, keeping his heart and soul entirely as well as solely devoted to the study of Kashmir Shaivism, though he eminently served and retired as the Head of the Department of Sanskrit and also Director of Sanskrit & Indological Studies from Kurukshetra University to join the Asiatic Society of Bengal as Mm. Gopinath Kaviraj Senior Research Professor.

May he leave to posterity the fruits of his lifelong researches in this field, this is my earnest prayer.

Govinda Gopal Mukhopadhyaya
Kolkata
June 8, 2006

Abbreviations

Āh	Āhnika
Br. Up	Bṛhadāraṇyaka Upaniṣad
IPV	Īśvara Pratyabhijñā Vimarśinī (Bhāskarī Ed)
IPVV	Īśvara Pratyabhijñā Vivṛti Vimarśinī (KSTS)
Jan. Man Vi	Janma-maraṇa-vicāra (KSTS)
MM	Mahārthamañjarī (KSTS)
MVT	Mālinī Vijaya Tantra (KSTS)
Par Car	Paramārtha Carcā
Par Sār	Paramārthasāra (KSTS)
Para Tṛim	Parātriṁśikā (RSTS)
Pr. Hḍ.	Pratyabhijñāhṛdayam (Adyar)
S D	Śivadṛṣṭi (KSTS)
Śiv Sū	Śivasūtra (KSTS)
Sp. Kā	Spanda Kārikā (KSTS)
Sp. Nir	Spanda Nirṇaya (KSTS)
STTS	Sattriṁśattattvasandoha (Kurukshetra)
Sva. Tan	Svacchanda Tantra (KSTS)
T A	Tantrāloka (KSTS)
T S	Tantrasāra (KSTS)
Vijbh	Vijñānabhairava (KSTS)
Ved. Sar	Vedāntasāra (Poona)

PREFACE

The distinguishing feature of Indian Philosophy in general is its pragmatic approach towards the problems of human life. It does not rest with merely postulating a metaphysical theory; it also formulates a way to reach the Supreme Goal in life. Every school of Indian thought, therefore, prescribes a mode of spiritual discipline commensurate with its own conception of the ultimate Reality, and this is given the name of Yoga. The yogic discipline thus constitutes an integral aspect of the metaphysical theory of all schools of Indian thought.

There were different schools of yogic thought in the pre-Patañjali era, though very little is known about them due to non-availability of literature pertaining to them. Therefore Patañjali is given the credit of systematising concepts relating to yogic practices that were formulated before him as well as providing the necessary metaphysical background. The yogic discipline prescribed by him became so popular that the then prevailing other modes or spiritual discipline could not gain currency. Hence, the system of Yoga became synonymous with *Pātañjala Yoga Darśana*.

The discoveries made by archaeologists at different prehistoric sites like Mohenjodaro, Harappa, Kalibangan, Lothal etc reveal that the people practised some kind of yoga even in these pre-historic times, as is evident from of the seals found there. The Tāntrika tradition, which appears to have some connection with the *Atharvaveda*, did exist in the beginning in the form of cults in which various modes of spiritual discipline dominated. The metaphysical theories in support of the spiritual goals visualised by the practitioners of Tantra Yoga developed much later, which is evident from the fact that the available Tāntrika literature is of much later date. It is significant to note that most Tāntrika texts pay more attention to the depiction of the *kriyā* aspect, the practical aspect — a fact which supports our hypothesis that the Tāntrika tradition, both Śaiva and Śākta, prevailed in the beginning only in the form of cult.

As a student of Indian philosophy and religion, I was attracted towards the study of Tantra Yoga while doing research on the spiritual discipline according to Kashmir Śaivism under the supervision of late Mahamahopādhyāya Dr Gopināth Kavirāj, a well-known savant and exponent of Tantrism. I studied some Tantric texts with him, which gave me insight to the mysteries of Tantra Yoga and inspired me to continue my study of the Śaiva and Śākta Tantras, which have many things in common.

In this book I have chosen to highlight a few important aspects related to the Tantra Yoga, e.g. the concepts of the highest spiritual Reality, man and his nature, the concept of *guru*, divine grace, initiation, the Supreme Goal, etc, which are important for a student of philosophy of religion to know. I have refrained from giving details of the Tantric practices, which are generally kept secret lest these should be misused. The Tāntrika texts are generally replete with such descriptions. My approach to Tantra Yoga has been intellectual and academic, hence I have tried to throw light on the philosophic implications of the various yogic practices and to unravel the mysteries contained therein. I have relied more on such Tāntrika texts as the *Mālinīvijayottara Tantra*, the *Svacchanda Tantra*, the *Vijñānabhairava Tantra*, the *Netra Tantra*, the *Tantrāloka* and the *Tantrasāra* as these give the metaphysical details underlying Tantra Yoga.

I have also made an attempt to give a brief account of the extent of Tantric literature in the first chapter entitled 'Tantra', its meaning, scope and extent. Vast Tantric literature was produced under the Śaiva and Śākta tradition but unfortunately most of it is either lost or remains unpublished.

I have used Sanskrit terms frequently but reluctantly, for want of suitable synonyms in English. The Tantras lean heavily to the mystical side and use such terminology which cannot be adequately translated into English. However, I have given English equivalents in parenthesis wherever possible, besides the Glossary at the end.

I consider it my duty to acknowledge the debt of my gratitude to my guru late Mahāmahopādhyāya Dr Gopināth Kavirāj who initiated me to the Tantric lore; to his valuable works for understanding the deep spiritual meaning underlying the various Tantric practices; to Sir John Woodroffe for his learned pioneering works in the field of Tantric studies.

I am also grateful to my teacher Dr. Govinda Gopal Mukhopadhyaya for inspiring me to undertake this work and showering his blessings. He has been pressing me to share with interested readers the knowledge I gained from my teachers and the study of abstruse texts over the years.

I express my gratefulness to Mr Alvaro Enterria, Publications Director, Indica Books, for carefully going through the manuscript and suggesting many improvements in the book. I am also thankful to Shri D.K. Jaiswal, Director of Indica Books, Varanasi, for kindly undertaking the publication of this book and seeing it through the press.

Last but not least, I am also thankful to my wife Mrs Dipika SenSharma for the support she has been giving in the production of this book.

I am conscious of my limitations, for which I solicit apology from my readers. Despite all care many errors in printing might have crept in, from which I crave their indulgence.

Deba Brata SenSharma
Kolkata

~CHAPTER I~

Tantra
Its Meaning, Scope and Extent

What is Tantra

Derived etymologically from the Sanskrit root Sanskrit *tan*, the term *tantra* primarily signifies 'elaboration' or 'extension',[1] and is therefore applied to denote that class of literature which elaborates or extends the frontiers of our knowledge.[2] This term was used in this non-technical sense for centuries as is evident from usages in such texts as the *Mahābhārata*,[3] where it has been used to denote some philosophical systems like the Nyāya Śāstra, Yoga Śāstra, Dharma Śāstra etc. Even Saṅkarācārya (8th cent. AD) in his *Śārīraka bhāṣya* has used this term to denote *śāstras* like Nyāya and Yoga, and has also included even the *smṛtis* in his list of Tantras.[4]

The term *tantra*, in the restricted and technical sense, is applied to that class of literature which is religious and mystical in content and abounds in magical words or incantations (*mantra*), which is believed to be capable of yielding spectacular results. The *Kāmikāgama* explains the meaning of the technical term *tantra* in the following words — "that which elaborates great things, consists of Truth (*tattva*) and mystical incantations (*mantra*) and saves (us from calamities and danger) is called Tantra."[5]

---

1 Cf. Monier Williams: *A Sanskrit-English Dictionary*. The lexicons generally have given several meanings.

2 *Tanyate vistāryate jñānamanena iti tantram.*

3 Cf. Upadhyaya, B: *Bhāratīya Darśana*, Varanasi, 1951, p. 542.

4 *Op. cit.*, Su. II, i, 1.

5 *Tenoti vipulānarthān tattva-mantra samanvitān trāṇam kurute yasmāt tantramityabhidhiyate*. Quoted in *Bhāratīya Darśana*, p. 542.

The Tantras generally are said to consist of the following — magical incantations (*mantras*), metaphysical principles and their philosophy (*tattva*), the nature of the world, initiatory rites, worship, various ceremonies or observances enjoined in the Tantras, mental and bodily discipline (*yoga*). The *Vārāhi Tantra* classifies the vast mass of Hindu Tantras under three broad heads, viz *Āgama*, *Yāmala* and *Tantra*. It enumerates seven salient features possessed by *Āgamas*, viz description of (i) creation (ii) dissolution, (iii) worship of some particular god or goddess, (iv) spiritual discipline (*sādhanakriyā*), (v) initiatory rites (*puraścaraṇa*), (vi) a group of six rites (*ṣaṭ karma*): *śānti* (propitiatory rite for averting evil), *vaśīkaraṇa* (rite for subduing and taming), *manana* (meditation), *ucāṭana* (magical rite for driving evil forces away), and (vii) *dhyānayoga* (profound meditation).[6]

The *Yāmalas* are said to possess eight distinguishing characteristics, viz (i) account of creation (*sṛṣti,*), (ii) position of planets and stars, (iii) daily rites (*nityakṛtya pratipādanam*), (iv) evolution (*krama*), (v) *sūtras*, (vi) distinction between *varṇas* (*varṇabheda*), (vii) distinction of caste (*jātibheda*), and (viii) duties of *āsrama*.[7] The *Tantras* are said to be characterised by innumerable distinguishing marks but the *Vārāhī Tantra* has enumerated as many as twenty-four marks, some of which are in common with those mentioned above. Among the additional distinguishing marks listed in the *Vārāhī Tantras*, mention may be made of the statement of *mantra* (magical incantations), *yantra* (magical diagrams), description of various gods and goddesses, holy places (*tīrthas*), performance of fasts (*vrata*), statement of distinction between holy and unholy, statement of the duties of the king (*rājadharma*) and of the common man (*vyavahāra*) and description of spiritual wisdom (*adhyātma varṇanam*) etc.[8]

---

6 Quoted by Baladeva Upadhyaya: *Bhāratīya Darśana*, Varanasi, 1950, p. 763.

7 *Sṛṣtiśca jyoṣtiākhyānaim nityakṛtyapratipādanam |*
kramasūtraṁ varṇabhedo jātibhedastathaiva ca |
yugadharmaśca samkhyāto yāmalasyāṣṭalakṣanam |

8 *Ibid.*

It may mentioned here that though the *Vārāhī Tantra* has specified certain characteristics or the distinguishing marks of the Tāntrika class of literature, all these salient features, as a matter of fact, are not found in all the Tantric texts. What is common to all the *Tantras* as a distinct class of religio-philosophical literature is their emphasis on the *Kriyā-yoga* or *sādhanakriyā* aspect and the abundance of mystic and esoteric elements and magical incantations or *mantras*.

Origin of the Tantras

Like the *Vedas*, the *Tantras* are traditionally believed to be eternal by their very nature, having emanated from the mouth of the Supreme Lord (*Parameśvara*). Abhinavagupta, in his *magnum opus* the *Tantrāloka*, describes in the following manner how the *Tantras* were revealed in the hoary past to the sages by the Supreme Lord:

"The All-transcending Word (*Parāvāk*) or Logos contains within it all the *Śāstras* (*Āgama* or *Tantra*) in super-sensuous 'seed form' (*bījarūpeṇa*). This Logos assumes the gross perceptible form of syllables or vocables in gradual steps. The first step towards materialisation is technically called '*paśyantī*' in which the two aspects of consciousness, viz *prakāśa* and *vimarśa* are completely merged, and the words and their meanings are fused together. In this stage the objects of perception appear as inseparably fused with the subject. In the succeeding step of *madhyamā*, the word and meaning appear as differentiated from one another, though not projected outside or expressible in gross vocables. The last step, technically called *vaikharī*, signalises the projection of what was contained in seed-form within the Logos when it becomes expressible in gross physical words." [9]

Thus *Śāstras* or *Tantras* are eternally existent in the form of *Parāvāk*, and their manifestation in gross form however is subject to certain conditions within the framework of time and space.

---

[9] *Tantrāloka* I, p. 34.

Looking from the historical point of view, the Tantric literature, as is available today, on the basis of its language and contents appears to be written in the post-upaniṣadic era, though there are indications available in the Vedic texts[10] to show the existence of a Tāntrika tradition as a parallel current to the Vedic tradition. Several *mantras* occurring in the *Ṛgveda* and the *Atharvaveda Saṁhitās* refer to certain esoteric doctrines and occult practices that were in vogue in those times. Some *Upaniṣads* also mention certain secret *vidyās* such as *Dahara Vidyā*,[11] *Madhu Vidyā*,[12] *Haṁsa Vidyā*,[13] etc, which conclusively prove the existence of the Tantric tradition. Some historians however trace the origin of Tantric lore to pre-Vedic times on the basis of archaeological finds discovered at different prehistoric sites, and connect it with the non-Aryan aborigines of this land, but in the present state of our knowledge, it is not possible to arrive at any definite conclusion in the absence of any other corroborative evidence except some artefacts discovered by the archaeologists at different sites.

Here, it would perhaps not be out of place to mention that, despite the prevalence of the Tantric tradition in some form or the other in the Vedic times, it was not very popular with the masses for a variety of reasons. The cult of sacrifice that developed soon after the 'visualisation' of the Truth in the form of Vedic *mantras* by the *ṛṣis* reigned supreme till the advent of Mahāvīra and Gautaṁa Buddha who vehemently criticised hollow ritualistic cult and emphasized the inner symbolic meaning of *mantra*, which was lost to lay people by that time. There thus developed a general public abhorrence against the cult of sacrifice.[14] The Tantric tradition, which had grown in the

---

[10] Cf. *Śatapatha Brāhmaṇa*, XI 11, 6, 13 which refers to *ātmayājī*. *Taittirīya Āraṇyaka* describes *cidyāga*.

[11] *Chāndogya* up. viii, 1-6.

[12] *Ibid* vii, 1-10, *Bṛhadāraṇyaka Upaniṣad*, II, 5.

[13] Cf *Sāyaṇabhāṣya* on the *RV. Vāmadeva Sūkta*, RV. iv, 40, 4, *Śukla YV*. X, 2; *Kaṭhopaniṣad* II, 2.

[14] Pañcaśikha's statement *Syāt svalpaḥ śaṅkāraḥ sapratyvamarśaḥ* etc quoted in the *Vyāsabhāṣya* on the *Yogasūtra*, II, 13; Also see *Sāṅkhya Tattva Kaumudī* Ka 1.

beginning in the form of certain rituals performed secretly by a few adepts outside the public gaze, also came to be looked down upon by people in the then prevailing anti-ritualistic atmosphere. In fact, so vehement was the outcry against ritualistic practices, Vedic or otherwise, that the Tantric rituals in general were considered to be unholy, and the person performing them was forbidden from entering into a sacrificial *paṇḍāl*.

Some scholars like P.C. Bagchi believe that the Tantric tradition had its origin in Tibet and China, and that it was introduced into India through Vajrayāna Buddhism.[15] This view appears to be a mere hypothesis in the absence of corroborative evidence.

Some scholars like Dr Gopinath Kaviraj are of the opinion that the Tāntrika cult developed hand in hand with the Buddhist Tantric tradition, of which Asaṅga is traditionally regarded as the founder. It is believed that Asaṅga, the famous Buddhist scholar, brought the *Tantravidyā* down to earth from the *Tuṣitta* heaven. Maitreyanātha, who was said to be a *siddha yogin*, was his teacher.[16]

According to another view, Hevajra was the founder of Tantric Buddhism, to whom the *Hevajra Tantra* is ascribed. He was followed by a host of Tantric writers among whom mention may be made of Sarorūpa, Vajra, Ānandavajra, Anaṅgavajra, Indrabhūti, etc. Their works on Tantric Buddhism are not available nowadays.[17]

Some scholars think that Nāgārjuna was the most important exponent of the Tantric cult in the Buddhist stream. There appears to be some truth in this view because Nāgārjuna hailed from Śrī Parvat or Dhānya Kaṅṭaka in Andhra Pradesh, which was a well-known seat for Tāntrika worship in the ancient period.[18]

Thus we find that the origin of the Tāntrika tradition is shrouded in the hoary past. In fact is is impossible for us in the present state of our knowledge to support or contradict any particular view about the origin of the *Tantras* and arrive at a definite conclusion.

---

[15] P.C. Bagchi: *Studies in Tantras*, p. 2.

[16] G.N. Kaviraj: *Tāntrika Sādhanā O Siddhānta* Vol. II, Burdwan, 1969, p. 22.

[17] *Ibid*, p. 43-44.

[18] *Ibid*, p. 22.

Scope of the Tāntrika cult

A study of the Tāntrika Buddhism in the historical perspective reveals that it existed in the hoary past in the form of a religious cult covering the entire length and breadth of the country. The existence of fifty-two centres of Tāntrika worship of the Divine Śakti in the form of the Mother Goddess, generally called the *Śāktapīṭhas*, bears ample testimony to its sweep in all the four corners of the country, which included Baluchistan.[19] According to an old tradition mentioned in the *Kalpasūtra* of Paraśurāma, the whole country was divided under three regions, viz *Viṣṇukrāntā*, *Aśvakrāntā* and *Rathakrāntā*.[20] The geographical limits of the different regions are indicated there. For instance, the *Viṣṇukrāntā* extended from the Vindhyas upto Chittagong in the east, including all the places in the northeastern region. The *Rathakrāntā* is said to cover the entire area in the north-western region that lay between the north of the Vindhyas up to Mahācīna or the modern Tibet in the north, while the *Aśvakrāntā* spread over the vast area from the Vindhyas up to the oceans in the south. According to another version recorded in the *Mahāsiddhisāra Tantra*,[21] *Aśvakrāntā* spread over the area from the river Karatoyā up to Java. A large number of centres for the propagation of Tāntrika cult — Śaiva, Śākta, Vaiṣṇava and Buddhist — developed within the three regions in the course of the centuries. Except for the account preserved in the ancient texts and the existence of Śākta temples dedicated to the worship of the Divine Mother at 52 places, there is no concrete evidence to support the existence of Tāntrika cults in the different regions mentioned above, on account of their being mostly oral in nature.

The Hindu Tāntrika tradition can be broadly classified under three heads, viz the Vaiṣṇava, the Śākta and the Śaiva, in accordance with their promoting the worship of Viṣṇu, Mother Goddess Śakti, and Śiva, in a deified form symbolically representing the Supreme Reality. Besides

---

[19] Sircar, D.C.: *The Śāktapīthas*, Calcutta.

[20] *Parasurāma Kalpasūtra*, Gaekwad Oriental Series, I, 9.

[21] Quoted in B. Upadhyaya: *Bhāratīya Darśana*, Varanasi, p. 57.

the Hindu Tāntrika tradition which, having emerged as an offshoot of the school of the Vaipulyavādins, not only spread in the country along the west and east coast in the South, Kashmir and Mahācīna in the north-western and northern part taking the form of Vajrayāna, but also percolated into the Hindu Tāntrika tradition. A comparative study of these two traditions would reveal the extent of their similarities.

As our present study of Tāntrika lore is concerned with the Śaiva and Śākta tantras, we shall confine ourselves to their study only. The Śaiva and Śākta traditions have so much in common with one another that it is very difficult to draw demarcating lines between the two.

Origin and development of the Tāntrika literature

We begin our brief survey of the Vaiṣṇava Tantras first represented by the *Pāñcarātra Āgamas* and the *Vaikhānasa Āgamas*. The Vaiṣṇava tāntrika tradition is a parallel tradition to the Śaiva and Śākta ones, therefore separate treatment of that tradition is necessary.

Both the *Pāñcarātra* and *Vatkhānasa Āgamas* were voluminous in form, but unfortunately a considerable part of the literature is now lost. According to Otto Schrader, the total number of *Pāñcarātra Saṁhitā* (*Āgama*) as mentioned in the *Kapiñjala Saṁhitā* was 215, of which only 13 are available now.[22] The best known among them are the *Ahirbudhnya Saṁhitā*,[23] the *Jayākahya Saṁhitā*,[24] the *Viṣṇu Saṁhitā*[25] and the *Sāttatva Saṁhitā*.[26] The *Lakṣmī Tantra* is another very popular Tāntrika text belonging to this tradition.

The Pāñcarātra School of Vaiṣṇava Tantra was closely related to the Ekāyana Śākhā (branch) of the *Śukla Yajurveda*.[27] The Vaikhānasa stream of Vaiṣṇava thought is also believed to be connected with the

---

[22] Schrader, Otto: *Introduction to the Pāñcarātra*, pp. 6-12.

[23] Published by Adyar Library, Madras.

[24] Published in Gaekwad Oriental Series, Baroda.

[25] Published in the Anantasayāna Series.

[26] Published from Kanchi.

[27] Cf. *Īśvarasaṁhitā*, I, 43; *Chand. Up*. VII, 12. Also See Nāgeśa in *Kānva-Śākhā Mahimnā Sāmaveda* (MS.), Dept. in Madras Oriental Literature.

Auraveya Śākhā of the *Kṛṣṇa Yajurveda*, to which reference has been made by Goutama in his *Dharmasūtra*,[28] *Bodhayana Dharma Śāstra*,[29] and the *Manusmṛti*.[30] Only four texts belonging to the Vaikhānasa School of the Vaiṣṇava Tāntrika tradition, namely the *Vaikhānasa Mantra Saṁhitā*, *Vaikhanāsa Gṛhyasūtra*, *Dharmasūtra* and *Śrauta-sūtra* are now available. The *Vaikhānasa Āgama* referred to by Mārīci has been published in the Anantasayana Sanskrit Series No. 12. It gives a detailed description of the philosophical tenets and the rituals of the Vaiṣṇava Tāntrika tradition.

According to ancient tradition, the spiritual wisdom contained in the various Tāntrika texts is eternal, existing as it does in the form of *parāvāk*, inseparably fused with the Supreme Reality on the transcendent level. It is beyond the reach of human mind. With the unfoldment of the totality of the universe, first in a subtle form of pulsations of Divine Śakti, then taking gross form, the Supreme Spiritual Wisdom existing in the subtle form of *Parāvāk*, symbolising the self-reflective experience by the Supreme Being, descended down as a parallel current to the Vedic one successively through two steps, namely, *paśyanti* and *madhyāmā*, to assume the gross form of *vaikharī*. According to the *Kulārṇava Tantra*,[31] the Tāntrika spiritual wisdom emanated in the hoary past from the five faces of Lord Śiva, viz *Īśāna*, *Tatpuruṣa*, *Sadyojāta*, *Aghora* and *Vāmadeva*,[32] pointing towards five different directions: Eastern, Western, Northern, Southern and the upward direction, technically called *āmnayas*.

Accordingly, the spiritual wisdom emanating from the eastern face of Lord Śiva and getting embodied in the form of Tāntrika texts is called *Pūrvamnāya*; the spiritual wisdom emanating from the southern face taking the form of Tāntrika texts is given the name *Dakṣiṇāmnāya*, the one emanating from the western face is called the *Paścimāmnāya* while the wisdom emanating from the northern face is called *Uttarāmnāya*. The spiritual wisdom emanating from

[28] *Op. Cit.*, III, 2.
[29] *Op. Cit.*, II, 6, 17.
[30] *Op. Cit.*, I, 6-7.
[31] *Op. Cit.*, *Ullāsa*, III, 7.
[32] Cf. Chatterjee, J.C.: *Kashmir Saivism*.

the upper face known as Vāmadeva, is considered most pure in form and is given the name *Ūrdhvāmnāya*. The *Kulārṇava Tantra* says that the Tantras belonging to the *Ūrdhāmnāya* are superior to those of other *āmnayas*, therefore most venerated. The *Tantrāloka* supports this view about the divine origination of the *Tantras*.[33]

Division of the Tāntrika tradition

It has been mentioned in the foregoing pages that the Hindu Tāntrika tradition can be broadly classified under three heads, namely the Vaiṣṇava, the Śaiva, and the Śākta. Each tradition has a considerable wealth of literature of its own to support and sustain its spiritual thought projections.

The extent of the Vaiṣṇava Tāntrika literature has already been mentioned under the heading 'Origin and development of Tāntrika literature'. Let us now turn our attention to the Śaiva and Śākta traditions, mentioning briefly the extent of the literature on which they lean for support, and their sub-schools which emerged in different parts of the country with the passage of time.

In this context, it is necessary to point out that the Śaiva and Śākta traditions have so much in common insofar as their spiritual thought projections and the mode of spiritual practices they prescribe are concerned, that it is very hazardous to draw with certainty a line of demarcation between them. The Śaiva and Śākta scriptures are inter-changeable. It is therefore safe to follow the scheme of classification of their literature available from the tradition.

Śaiva Tāntrika literature

According to one tradition, the total number of Śaiva Tantras is 28, which includes 10 Śaivāgamas or Śaiva Tantras, and 18 Raudrāgamas. The *Kiraṇāgama*[34] gives the names of ten Śaivagamas as well as their subdivisions and extent, which are as follows:

[33] Cf. *Tantrāloka* I, 35 Vivṛti com. thereon.

[34] A *Raudrāgama* available in MS form in Nepal. This manuscript, bearing the date 924 A.D. was noted by Mm. H.P. Shastri. See Nepal Durbar Cat, Vol. II, p. 20.

i) *Kāmikāgama* or *Kāmaja*[35] — The text is now lost but its quotations are found in the commentaries on other Śaiva works.

ii) *Yogaja* — It was divided into five parts and is said to contain one lakh (100,000) verses, now lost.

iii) *Cintā* or *Cintyā* — It was comprised of six parts and contained one lakh verses, now lost.

iv) *Karaṇāgama* — It contained seven parts and is said to have one crore (ten millions) verses, now lost.

v) *Ajitāgama* — It was divided into four parts and contained one lakh verses.

vi) *Sudīptaka or Dīpta* — It contained nine subdivisions and had one lakh verses, now lost.

vii) *Sūkṣma* — It had no divisions but is said to contain one *padma* (10,000 billions) verses, now lost.

viii) *Sahasra* — It was comprised of ten parts, now lost.

ix) *Suprabheda* — It had no divisions but is said to contain three crore verses.

x) *Amśumāna* — It had ten divisions.

All these *Śaivagamas* are believed to propagate a dualist philosophy (*dvaita*).

Here it may be pointed out that the list of *Śaivāgamas* given in the *Śrīkaṇṭhī Saṁhitā*[36] is slightly different, as it does not contain the name of *Suprabheda Tantra*. In its place the name of *Mukuṭāgama* has been mentioned. These have also been mentioned by Jayaratha in his commentary on the *Tantrāloka*.[37] The *Mṛgendra Tantra*[38] also gives the names of the ten *dvaita Śaiva Tantras* listed above.[39]

---

35 Jayaratha in his commentary on the *Tantrāloka* mentions this name on the authority of *Śrīkaṇṭha Saṁhitā* (T.A. I, 35).

36 The name of this Śaiva text, now lost, has been mentioned by Jayaratha in his com. on *Tantrāloka*, T.A. 1.35 & I 42.3.

37 *Op. Cit.*, Vol. I, p. 39.

38 See Introduction, portion p. 2 published in Kashmir Series of Texts.

39 See also Farquhar: *Outline of Religious Literature in India*, p. 193.

The eighteen *Raudrāgamas* which are said to propagate monistic-cum-dualistic philosophy are as follows:

1. *Vijaya*, 2. *Niḥśvāsa*, 3. *Pārameśvara*, 4. *Prodgīta*, 5. *Mukhabimba*, 6. *Siddha*, 7. *Sanātana*, 8. *Narasiṁha*, 9. *Candrāṁśu* or *Candrahāsa*, 10. *Vīrabhadra*, 11. *Svayam-bhuva*, 12. *Viraja*, 13. *Kauravya*, 14. *Makuṭa* or *Mukuṭa*, 15. *Kirana*, 16. *Galita*, 17. *Āgneya*, 18. Name not known. All these *Raudrāgamas* except the *Kiraṇāgama* are now lost.

On the authority of *Śrīkaṇṭhī Saṁhitā*, Jayaratha in his commentary on the *Tantrāloka*[40] has enumerated the list of 18 *Raudrāgamas* preaching *dvaita* Śaiva philosophy. This list is slightly different from that given above, as it contains the names of the *Raurava*, *Vimala*, *Visara* and *Sauraveya Āgamas* in place of the *Virakta*, *Kauravya*, *Makuṭa* and *Āgneya*. All these *Āgamas* exist only in name, but as Abhinavagupta in his *Tantrāloka* has quoted from some of the *Raudrāgamas*, viz *Kiraṇa*,[41] *Raurava*[42] and *Siddha Tantras*,[43] this goes to vouchsafe for their existence at least in his time.

It may be mentioned here that *Brahma Yāmala Tantra*, a Bhairava Tantra available in Nepal Durbar Library in manuscript form,[44] gives a different list of *Raudrāgamas*, which is as follows:

1. *Vijaya*, 2. *Niḥśvāsa*, 3. *Svāyambhuva*, 4. *Vātula*, 5. *Vīrabhadra*, 6. *Raurava*, 7. *Vīrasa*, 8. *Candrajñāna*, 9. *Prodgīta*, 10. *Lalitā*, 11. *Siddhisāra Tantra*, 12. *Sarvodgīta*, 13. *Kiraṇa*, 14. *Pārameśvara*. Another version of these names with some additions and modifications is found in the *Uttarasūtra* of *Niḥśvāsatattva Saṁhitā*, a manuscript written in the Gupta script of the eight century A.D. deposited in the Nepal Durbar Library. These are *Niḥśvāsa*, *Svāyambhuva*, *Vātula*,

---

[40] T.A. Vol. I, p. 35.

[41] *Ibid*, Vol. I, p. 116, Vol. III, Vol. IV, p. 84, Vol. VI, V. 9, p.45.

[42] *Ibid,* Vol. V, Ah. 8, p. 30 & 74.

[43] *Ibid*, Vol. V, p. 256.

[44] See H.P. Sastri: *Nepal Durbar Cat. of MSS*, Vol. II, p. 60.

Vīrabhadra, *Raurava*,[45] *Mukuṭa*,[46] *Vīrasa* (*Viresa*?) *Candrahāsa*, *Jñāna*, *Mukhabimba*, *Prodgīta*, *Lalitā*, *Siddha*, *Sanātana*, *Sarvodgīta*, *Kiraṇa*, and *Pārameśvara*. It may be pointed out here that the names of all the eighteen *Āgamas* are not available in any of the above-mentioned texts.

The *Kāmikāgama*[47] mentions the names of eighteen *Raudrāgamas* along with ten *Śaivāgamas*, which are said to have emanated from the five faces of the Supreme Lord, Śiva. It has been said there that the *Kāmika*, *Yogaja*, *Cintā* or *Cintyā*, *Kāraṇa* and *Ajita* — this group of five *Śaivāgamas* emanated from the face of Lord Śiva called Sadyojāta; the *Dīpta*, *Sūkṣma*, *Sahasra Aṁśumata* or *Aṁśuman* and *Suprabheda* — these five *Śaivāgamas* appeared from the face called Vāmadeva, while *Vijaya*, *Niḥśvāsa*, *Svayambhuva*,[48] *Āgneya* and *Vīra* — these five *Raudrāgamas* did so from the face called Aghora; the *Raurava*, *Mukuṭa*, *Vimalāgma Candrakāntā* and *Vimba* — these five *Raudrāgamas* emanated from the face called Īśāna; *Prodgīta*, *Lalita*, *Siddha*, *Sanātana*, *Sarvokta*, *Pārameśvara*, *Kiraṇa*[49] and *Vātula* — these eight *Raudrāgamas* originated from the face called Tatpuruṣa.

Here it may be mentioned that these eighteen *Raudrāgamas* are venerated by the Pāśupatas as the authentic *Āgamas*, since they also propound the dualist cum-monistic philosophy.

In addition to the above mentioned twenty-eight Śaiva Tantras advocating dualistic and dualist-cum-monistic Śaiva philosophy, there are a group of sixty-four Bhairava Tantras which preach purely monistic Śaiva philosophy. *Śrīkaṇṭha Saṁhitā* has given the names

---

45 Quoted by Mādhavācārya in *Sarva Darśana Saṁgraha* under *Śaiva Darśana* p. 77 (Jīvānanda edition).

46 Quoted by Abhinavagupta in *Parātrimśika Vivaraṇa*, p. 237.

47 The text of *Kāmikāgama* in its original form is lost. It has been said that the available text of the *Mṛgendrāgama* forms a part of the lost *Kāmikāgama*. See *Mṛgendra Tantra*, introduction and Jayaratha's com. thereon. Abhinavagupta has quoted from this *Āgama* in his *Tantrāloka*, Ah. I, p. 97 & 104; Ah. VI, p. 28.

48 Quoted by Abhinavagupta in his *Īśvarapratyabhijñā Vim.*, Vol. II, p. 200.

49 Quoted by Jayaratha in his Com. in T.A. I, p. 42-43. Also see MVV, p. 38.

of these Tantras under eight groups, each group comprising eight Tantras. The names of these Tantras are given below under eight heads.

1. Bhairavāṣṭaka or *Bhairava Tantras* [50]

a) *Svacchandabhairava*

b) *Caṇḍa Bhairava*

c) *Krodha Bhairava* [51]

d) *Unmattabhairava*

e) *Aṣṭāngabhairava*

f) *Mahocchuṣma Bhairava* [52]

g) *Kapāliśa Bhairava*

h) Name not known [53]

2. *Yāmalāṣṭaka* or *Yāmala Tantras*

a) *Brahma Yāmala*

b) *Viṣṇu Yāmala*

c) *Svacchanda Yāmala* [54]

d) *Ruru Yāmala* [55]

e) *Atharvaṇa Yāmala*

f) *Vetāla Yāmala*

g) *Rudra Yāmala*

h) Name not known

---

[50] Abhinavagupta refers to this group as Bhairavakula in his MV. See Also T.A., Ah. XIII, p. 82.

[51] Abhinavagupta refers to *Rudrabhairava Tantra* in MVV p. 38, which is probably the same as *Krodhabhairava Tantra*.

[52] Quotation from this Tantra referred to as *Ucchusma Śāstra* are available in Abhinavagupta's works, eg. *Tantrasāra*, p. 32.

[53] Dr. K.C. Pandey in his book *Abhinavagupta, An Historical and Philosophical Study* wrongly gives the name of eight Tantras as Bhairava (p. 78 ff). Bhairava is the name of the group of Tantras, and not a particular Tantra.

[54] The *Svacchanda Yāmala* and *Svacchanda Tantra* are probably the same. The latter is available in printed form.

[55] The name of *Raurava Śāstra* occurs in the *Tantrasāra*, p. 186. It is probably the same as the *Ruru Yāmala*. See also T.A. Ah. VIII, p. 30 & 74.

3. *Matāṣṭaka* or *Mata Tantras*
   a) *Rakta*
   b) *Lampaṭa*
   c) *Lakṣmīmata*
   d) *Cūlikā*
   e) *Piṅgalā Mata*
   f) *Utphallaka Mata*
   g) *Viśvādya Mata*
   h) Name not known
4. *Maṅgalāṣṭaka* or *Maṅgala Tantras*
   a) *Picubhairavī*
   b) *Tantrabhairavī*
   c) *Tata*
   d) *Brāhmī Kalā*
   e) *Vijaya*
   f) *Maṅgala* [56]
   g) *Candra*
   h) *Sarvamaṅgalā*
5. *Cakrāṣṭaka* or *Cakra Tantras*
   a) *Mantracakra*
   b) *Varṇacakra*
   c) *Śakticakra*
   d) *Kālacakra*
   e) *Bindu Cakra*
   f) *Nāda Cakra*
   g) *Gūhya Cakra* [57]
   h) *Pūrṇacakra* [58]

---

[56] Abhinavagupta has quoted from *Maṅgala Śāstra* in his T.A., Vol. III Ah. V, p. 374, which is probably the same as *Maṅgala Tantra*.

[57] K.C. Pandey in his book ***Abhinavagupta: An Historical and Philosophical Study*** has given the name as *Guhyacakra* (See p. 79). Abhinavagupta has quoted from *Guhyayoginī Tantra* in his *Parā Triṁśikā Vivaraṇa* (p. 120) which could be the same as the above mentioned Tantra.

[58] Dr. K.C. Pandey has given the name as *Khacakra*. See ***Abhinavagupta: An Historical and Philosophical Study***, p. 79.

6. *Bahurūpaṣṭaka* or *Bahurūpa Tantras*
   a) *Andhaka*
   b) *Rurubheda*
   c) *Aja*
   d) *Mūla*
   e) *Varṇabheda*
   f) *Viḍaṅga*
   g) *Mātrādana*
   h) *Jvālina*

7. *Vāgiśāṣṭaka* or *Vāgīśa Tantras*
   a) *Bhairavī*
   b) *Citraka*
   c) *Haṁsa*
   d) *Kadambikā*
   e) *Hrilekhā*
   f) *Vidyullekhā*
   g) *Candra lekhā*
   h) *Vidyumat*

8. *Śikhaṣṭaka* or *Śikhā Tantras*
   a) *Bhairavī Śikhā*
   b) *Vīṇaśikhā* [59]
   c) *Viṇamani*
   d) *Sammoha* [60]
   e) *Dāmara* [61]
   f) *Atharvaka*
   g) *Kabandha*
   h) *Śiraśccheda*

---

[59] Dr. P.C. Bagchi in his *Studies in Tantra* (Vol. I, p. 2) has mentioned the names of four Tantras, viz *Bīṇaśikhā Sammoha*, *Śiraśccheda* and *Nayottara*, which were taken to Cambodia in 802 A.D. Bīnaśikhā appears to be the corrupt form of the above mentioned tantra.

[60] The name of this Tantra figures in the list of Tantras believed to have been taken to Cambodia.

[61] Abhinavagupta has referred to *Dāmara Tantra* in his comm. on *Mal. Vij. Tan*, p. 16.

We come across the names of some Tantras in Abhinavagupta's works, which have either been quoted or referred to as authorities there. The names of these Tantras do not figure in the above mentioned list of *advaita* Śaiva Tantras. There are *Bharga Śikhā*,[62] *Nandīśikhā*,[63] *Nitya Tantra*,[64] *Siddha Tantra*,[65] *Bhairava Tantra*,[66] *Rudra Tantra*,[67] etc. It may be mentioned here that *advaita śaivācāryas* belonging to the Ṭrika School venerate *Malivijayottara Tantra*, *Svacchanda Tantra*, *Vijñāna Bhairava*, *Mṛgendra*, *Mātaṅga Tantra* and *Netra Tantra* (all of them have been published from Kashmir). Some of these Tantras, e.g. *Svacchanda*, *Netra*, *Vijñāna Bhairava* and *Mātaṅga*, have been commented upon by Śaiva writers of Kashmir such as Kṣemarāja and Śivopadhyāya. Some Tantra texts such as *Ucchuṣma Bhairava*, *Ānanda Bhairava*,[68] *Niḥśvāsa Tantra*,[69] *Svayambhuva Tantra*,[70] *Rudrayāmala* have been frequently referred to or quoted as authorities, though they are either lost or remain unpublished, available only in manuscript form.

Śaiva Tāntrika schools

Based on the corpus of Śaiva Tantric texts, the following schools of Śaiva thought emerged and developed in different times in different parts of the country. K.C. Pandey in his lengthy introduction to Bhāskari Vol. III has listed eight Śaiva schools, viz Pāśupata, Lakulīśa-pāśupata, Śaiva Siddhānta, Vīraśaiva, Nandikeśvara Śaiva, Raseśvara Śaiva, Trika Śaiva and the Viśiṣṭādvaita Śaiva of Śrīkaṇṭha. Of these,

---

62 Referred to in *Parā Triṁśikā Viv*. p. 235, M.V.V. p. 17.

63 Referred to in the *Tantrasāra*, p. 27.

64 Mentioned in *Tantrasāra*.

65 *Ibid*, p. 187.

66 Quoted in T.A., Vol. I. Ah. I. 256.

67 Quoted in T.A. Vol. VII, Ah. XIII, p. 183. It may be the same as the *Vijñānabhairava Tantra* published in Kashmir Series of Texts.

68 Now lost.

69 Prof. P.C. Bagchi thinks that the MS of *Niḥśavāsa tattva Saṁhitā* deposited in the Nepal Durbar Library is probably the same as *Niḥśvasa Tantra* which is also found in the list of *Raudrāgamas*.

70 Referred to by Somānanda in S.D. III, 13-15.

the Pāśupata and the Lakulīśa-Pāśupata are the most ancient ones for which some historical evidence is available. But the Śaiva Siddhānta, Vīraśaiva and the Trika Śaiva, which emerged at a much later date, possess rich literature and many followers even today.

Mādhavācarya in his *Sarvadarśana Saṁgraha* has summarised the metaphysical doctrines of Pratyabhijñā (a constituent stream of the Trika school of Śaivism), Raseśvara Darśana and the Siddhānta Śaiva Darśana, while Haribhadra Sūri in his *Ṣaḍdarśana Samuccaya* has merely referred to the Pāśupata School. The Lakulīśa Pāśupata School was founded by Lakulīśa, a historical person according to archaeological evidence, the Nandikeśvara Śaiva and the Viśiṣṭādvaita Śaiva were founded by Śrīkaṇṭha have limited literature, the Vīraśaiva school is very popular even in modern Karnataka and has enough literature both in Sanskrit and in Kạnnada language.

Mm. Gopinath Kaviraj has listed thirteen Śaiva schools in addition to the above ones which also emerged from the Tantric thought current. These are: Kāpālikas, Kālāmukhas, Kāruṇika Śaiva, Kālānala, Jangama Raudra, Bhairava, Bhaṭṭa, Mahāvratins, Vāmaka, Kṣapaṇaka and Krama. With the exception of the Krama School, all other schools of Śaivism are known only through the references in different texts.

Vācaspati Miśra has enumerated four thought currents of Śaivism (*Māheśvara darśana*) which includes the Kāpalikas. Yāmunācārya has mentioned the Kāpalikas under Śaiva schools. The *Śiva Purāṇa* and the *Vāmana Purāṇa* have mentioned that Kāpālikas were seen moving about in good number in that period. Śrī Harṣa in his *Naiṣadha-carita* refers to some Siddhāntins but does not explain who they were. The well-known Sanskrit allegorical drama, *Prabodha Candrodaya* also mentioned the Somasiddhāntins, which has been explained by its commentator Rucikara as *Saha Umayā vartate iti Soma tasya siddhānta* (the school which advocates the existence of Śiva with Umā (Pārvatī). Raghuttama in his *Bhāṣya Candrikā* on the *Nyāya-bhāṣya* mentions the Soma School of Śaivas, which goes on to show its importance as well as popularity even in the 17th Century.

An inscription dated 620 A.D. found at Igatpuri mentions Mahāvratins for whom arrangements for food, etc were made at Kapāleśvara temple. The Mahāvratins also figure in the *Śivapurāṇa* and the *Svāyambhuva Āgama*. Mm. Gopinath Kaviraj has expressed the opinion that probably the Somasiddhāntins, Kāpālikas and Mahāvratins were all the same, and that different names were given to them in different times. But in the absence of literature belonging to them, it is not possible to arrive at some definite conclusion.

The Krama School was a very powerful school which prevailed in Kashmir before the rise of the Trika School in the early 8th century A.D. A lot of literature belonging to this Śaiva school exists even today. Abhinavagupta, one of the greatest exponents of the Trika School, incorporated their metaphysical thought in his exposition of Trika philosophy, thereby enriching the Trika thought. The *Mahārthamañjarī* of Maheśvarānanda (12th cent. A.D.) is the principal text which describes the main tenets of the Krama School of thought. Abhinavagupta, who lived before Maheśvarānanda, wrote two small works, *Kramastotra* and *Kramkeli*, in which he gives in brief the cardinal doctrines of this school, but these are now lost. The *Parimala* commentary on the *Mahārthamañjarī* mentions a number of works dealing with this tradition, viz *Mahārthodaya*, *Saṁvidullāsa*, *Kramasūkta*, *Pādukodaya*, *Parāstotra*, *Mukundabali*, *Krama Vallī* etc. From the same commentary, we come to know that Mahāprakāśa, the teacher of Maheśvarānanda, wrote two books, viz *Kramavāsanā* and *Ṛjuvimarśinī* which are now lost.

Śākta Tāntrika literature

Like the Śaiva tradition, the Śākta tradition too has a very rich literature which is evident from seven lists of 64 Tantras each mentioned in texts like *Vāmakeśvara Tantra*, Lakṣmīdhara's commentary on the *Saundaryalaharī* of Śaṅkarācārya, *Toḍalottara Tantra*, Bhaskararāya's commentary and three lists provided by *Siddhisāra Tantra*.

Śaṅkarācārya in his well-known work *Saundarya Laharī* has referred to 64 Tantras which were said to be instrumental in Lord Śiva acquiring supernormal powers (*siddhis*) to subjugate this world.[71]

The names of the 64 Tantras referred to by Śankarācārya figure in *Catuḥsati*.[72] Śaṅkarācārya himself is credited with authorship of one Tantra, called *Kādimākhya Tantra*, which he is said to have written following the orders of Goddess Pārvatī.[73] In this Tantra, he describes the way to attain the highest goal in life.

Lakṣmīdhara in his commentary on the *Saundaryalaharī* throws light on the contents of the 64 Tantras referred to by Śaṅkarācārya which, in general, deal with the way leading to the acquisition of certain supernormal powers or *siddhis*. For instance, the *Mahāmāyā Tantra* and the *Śāmbara Tantra* first describe the manner in which the illusory world is created by the power of Māyā Śakti, designated here as *Mohinī Vidyā*, corresponding to the hypnotism of modern times, and then lays down the spiritual discipline for acquiring this power. The *Yoginījāla* and the *Śāmbara Tantra* describe the way to make one *tattva* appear as some other *tattva*, e.g. *pṛthvītattva* appear as *jala tattva* or viceversa. It thus teaches a kind of magic (*indrajāla vidyā*). *Siddhī Bhairava*, *Batukabhairava*, *Kaṅkāla Bhairava*, *Kālabhairava*, *Kālāgnibhairava*, *Yoginī Bhairava*, *Mahābhairava* and *Śānti Bhairava* — these eight Bhairava Tantras describe the ways leading to the acquisition of worldly treasures (*nidhi vidyā*), and probably this group belongs to the Kāpalika stream of the Tāntrika tradition.[74]

A group of eight Bahurūpa Tantras, viz *Brāhmī*, *Māheśvarī*, *Kaumārī*, *Vaiṣṇavī*, *Vārāhī*, *Camuṇḍī*, *Śivadūtī*, etc., discusses the eight kinds of *mātṛkā śaktis* (aspects of the Divine Śakti) and therefore, appear to be Śākta Tantras. In this group, some Tantras like *Brāhmī*, *Vārāhī*, *Māheśvarī* are available. There is a group of eight Yāmala

---

[71] *Saundarya Laharī*, V. 31.

[72] Cf. G. Kaviraj: *Tantra O Āgamasaster Digdarśana*, p. 58.

[73] Cf. Saubhagyavardhini Com. the *Ānandalaharī*.

[74] Kaviraj, G.N.: *Tantra O Āgamasaster Digdarśana*, Calcutta, p. 58f.

Tantras which deal which *kāyasiddhi*, i.e. making the physical body develop supernormal powers by following a certain mode of disciplines. This was later on emphasised by Haṭhayogins and the followers of the Nātha cult.[75] The *Candrajñāna Tantra* is one of the well-known Tantras which discuss 16 *vidyās* as admitted also by the Kāpālikas, and it lays down the way to achieve them. Incidentally, it may be mentioned that it is different from its namesake, another *Candrajñāna* which belongs to the Vedic stream.

The *Mālinīvidyā* and *Mahāsammohana* are two well-known Tantras, the former describing the way to acquire the superhuman power of floating even in the sea, the latter dealing with the acquisition of hypnotic powers by performing such acts as cutting off the tongue of a child and offering it to the Goddess, etc.[76]

A group of five Tantras, viz *Vāmajuṣṭa*, *Mahādeva*, *Vātula*, *Vātulottara* and *Kāmika*, are said to describe certain modes of worship or practices whereby these appear to belong to certain non-Vedic sects not known at present. In this group, the *Kāmika* and *Vātula* are well known. Certain Tantras like *Hṛdbheda Tantra*, *Tantrabheda* and *Guhyabheda* are said to describe certain rites which are connected with the way to ascend to the higher planes of existence through *ṣaṭa-cakrabheda*, and therefore appear to be connected with the Kāpālika sect, while the *Tantrabheda* and *Guhyabheda* are said to describe the way to snatch through secret means the superhuman Tantric powers of a person. The *Kālavāda* and *Kubjikā Tantras* deal with certain rites relating to *Vāmācāra*, such as sanctification of the vessel for drinking, etc. The *Mulottara Tantra*, *Vīṇākhya Tantra* and *Toḍolottara Tantra* are said to deal respectively with *rasa-siddhi* (sanctification of *rasas*) *Yoginīsiddhi* (subjugation of a *yoginī* called Vīṇā for employing her for various works) *Añjana* and *Pādukāsiddhis*, etc. The *Todalottara Tantra* is believed to deal with the way to obtain a glimpse of 64080 *yakṣinīs* (celestial damsels), while the *Pañcāmṛta Tantra* is said to describe certain rites related to the Kāpālika sect.

[75] *Ibid*, p. 58f.

[76] *Ibid*, p. 58 f.

Most of the 64 Tantras enumerated above are now lost to us, but whatever idea we get about the contents of these Tantras is based on Lakṣmīdhara's commentary on the *Saundarya Laharī*. Lakṣmīdhara calls these *Tantras* non-Vedic for two reasons. Firstly, these are mainly meant for the lower class of people, viz the *śūdras* who do not undergo any purificatory rites (*saṁskāras*), and secondly, these aim at the acquisition of supernormal powers by following certain prescribed rites. Thus the primary concern of these Tantras appears to be material upliftment rather than spiritual progress, which is the goal of human life.

It has been stated in the *Saundarya Laharī* that the name of *Svacchanda Tantra* has deliberately been omitted from the list of 64 Tantras enumerated above. The reason for this omission is that it cannot be classed with these Tantras on account of the fact that it has a bias for spirituality, which is totally absent in other Tantras. There is difference of opinions about the name of the Tantra left out in the list. Bhāskararāya, in his commentary *Setubandha*, has suggested the name of *Vāmakeśvara Tantra*, while some other writers are of the opinion that the *Tantrarāja* has been deliberately left out from the above list. It may be mentioned that both are well-known Tantras, which have been oft quoted. The *Tantrarāja Tantra* is available in print.[77]

The *Toḍala Tantra*[78] gives yet another list of 64 Tantras different from the above one. The names of these Tantras also appear in the list provided by Sarvānanda Āgamavagīśa in his *Sarvollāsa Tantra*.[79] Hence these Tantras appear to be of a later origin than those mentioned in the older texts, such as *Catuḥśaṣṭhi* or *Śrīkaṇṭhī Saṁhitā*. A large number of these Tantras are available either in manuscript or in published form, a fact which testifies for their later origin. We give here below the names of these Tantras.

---

77 Ed. by Woodroffe.

78 Ed. by Bhadrasila Sharma. Also available in Bengali characters in Calcutta.

79 Pub. by Basumati Press, Calcutta.

1. *Kālī Tantra* [80]
2. *Muṇḍamālā Tantra*
3. *Tārātantra* [81]
4. *Nirvāṇa Tantra* [82]
5. *Śivasāra Tantra*
6. *Vīratantra*
7. *Nidarśana Tantra*
8. *Latārcana Tantra*
9. *Toḍala Tantra* [83]
10. *Nīla Tantra*
11. *Rādhā Tantra*
12. *Vidyā Sāra Tantra*
13. *Bhairava Tantra*
14. *Bhairavī Tantra*
15. *Siddheśvara Tantra*
16. *Mātṛkābheda Tantra* [84]
17. *Sāmaya Tantra*
18. *Guptasādhana Tantra*
19. *Māyā Tantra*
20. *Mahāmāyā Tantra*
21. *Akṣaya Tantra*
22. *Kumārī Tantra*
23. *Kulārṇava Tantra* [85]
24. *Kālikā Kāla Sarvasva Tantra*
25. *Kālikākalpa Tantra*
26. *Vārāhī Tantra* [86]
27. *Yoginī Tantra* [87]

---

[80] Ed. by Bhadrasila Sharma. [81] *Ibid.*

[82] Ed. by Nityanand Smrtitirth, Calcutta, 1878.

[83] Ed. Pancanana Shastri, Calcutta, 1978.

[84] Ed. Hemanta Kumar Tarkatirtha, Calcutta, 1978.

[85] Ed. by Bhadrasila Sharma; also ed. by Arthur Avalon, Delhi, 1975.

[86] Now lost.

[87] Published from Calcutta 1978 ed., Sarvesvaranath Sarasvati.

28. *Yoginī Hṛdaya* [88]
29. *Sanatkumāra Tantrā*
30. *Tripurasāra Tantra*
31. *Yoginī Vijaya Tantra*
32. *Mālinī Tantra* [89]
33. *Kukkuṭa Tantra*
34. *Śrīgaṇeśa Tantra*
35. *Bhūtatantra*
36. *Uḍḍiśa Tantra* [90]
37. *Kāmadhenu*
38. *Uttama Tantra*
39. *Vīrabhadra Tantra*
40. *Vāmakeśvara Tantra* [91]
41. *Kulcuḍāmaṇi Tantra*
42. *Bhavacuḍāmaṇi Tantra*
43. *Jñānarṇaya Tantra* [92]
44. *Varada Tantra*
45. *Tantra Cintāmaṇi Tantra*
46. *Vāṇīvilāsa Tantra*
47. *Haṁsa Tantra*
48. *Cidambara Tantra*
49. *Pheṭkārinī Tantra*
50. *Nityā Tantra*
51. *Uttara Tantra*
52. *Nārāyaṇī Tantra*
53. *Urdhvāmnāya Tantra*
54. *Jñānadīpa Tantra*
55. *Gautamīya Tantra*

---

[88] Published.

[89] Published.

[90] Published in Bengali characters, Calcutta.

[91] Published in Bengali characters.

[92] Ed. by Bhadrasila Sharma.

56. *Niruttara Tantra* [93]
57. *Garjana Tantra*
58. *Kubjikā Tantra* [94]
59. *Tantra Muktāvalī*
60. *Bṛhat Śrīkarma Tantra*
61. *Svatantra Tantra*
62. *Yoni Tantra*
63. *Kāmākhya Tantra* [95]
64. Now not known.

It may mentioned here that the *Dasarathi Tantra* in Chapter II provides us with another list of 64 Tantras, different from the earlier ones. This Tantra is available in manuscript form in the India Office Library and bears the date of 1676 Śaka era (1754 A.D.).

For centuries, the Tantric texts and practices remained confined within a narrow group of *sādhakas* who had been initiated to the secret lore of Tantras, so that it could never gain currency among the masses or attract the appreciation from the elite who always demanded rationale or logical explanations for everything propagated in the Tantra. The Tantric practices were also misused by unscrupulous *sādhakas* and misunderstood by people, which contributed to the development among people of a general abhorrence and antipathy for the Tantras and its practices. This eventually caused the rapid disappearance of a vast mass of Tantric literature from India, and a gradual drying up of the Tantric tradition. But it must be admitted in fairness that, though most of the Tantric texts are not available today, they have left an indelible mark on our present-day religious literature. Even the mode of daily worship by the devout Hindus and the performance of religious rites bear the imprint of certain Tantric practices which got percolated into their day-to-day religious life.

---

[93] Ed. Dinanath Tripathi, Calcutta, 1978.

[94] Published from Calcutta.

[95] Ed. by Jyoti Lal Das, Calcutta, 1978.

Śākta Tāntrika schools

We have given in the foregoing pages an idea of the enormous wealth of literature produced by the Śākta Tradition. We have seen seven lists of 64 Tantras provided to us by different works, most of them uncommon. As most of the Tantric texts mentioned in these lists are not available now in any form, it is extremely difficult to come to any definite conclusion. In this connection mention may be made that Abhinavagupta in his *magnum opus*, the *Tantrāloka*, as well as Jayaratha in his *vivṛti* commentary thereon, have made use of many of these texts. Jayaratha quoted from as many as 300 Tantra texts, both Śaiva and Śākta, the majority of them now lost. Pandit Vrajaballabha Dwivedi, under the direction of Mahāmahopādhyāya Pandit Gopināth Kavirāj, has collected these quotations and published them under several volumes called *Luptāgamasaṁgraha*. The writer of these lines came across one text called *Candrajñāna* quoted by Jayaratha which figures in some of the seven lists of Śaiva-Śākta Tantras mentioned above. He also came across two manuscripts of the *Candrajñāna* from two different places, but he was surprised to read the colophon given at the end of the manuscripts which tells us that it is a part of a larger text named *Candrahāsa Saṁhitā*, a text which is not mentioned in any of the lists referred to above. This is indeed very puzzling.

Since the emphasis on the Śākta tradition is more on the worship (*upāsanā*) by follower-devotees of the different deified forms of the Divine Śakti, technically called the *Mahāvidyās*, ten principal schools developed in course of time within the Śākta fold. According to the *Gandharva Tantra*, the ten *Mahāvidyās* are Kālī, Tārā, Ṣoḍaśī (or Śrīvidyā or Tripurasundarī), Bhuvaneśvarī, Bhairavī, Chinnamastā, Dhumāvatī, Bagalā, Mātaṅgī, and Kamalā, arranged in a particular order. These schools of Śakti-worship prevailed in different parts of the country, some confined to limited pockets, some spread throughout the length and breadth of the country. Every school of the Śākta tradition has some literature describing the concept and form of its particular Deity, and the mode of the *upāsanā* (worship) to be followed by her devotees to realise the ultimate Goal in life. We propose to give a brief account of these schools, their sub-schools and the literature involved under the following paragraphs.

i) Goddess Kālī

Goddess Kālī is a pre-eminent form of the Divine Śakti who is popular in different parts of the country under different names. According to the *Parātantra* (an unpublished text containing 4 chapters), Goddess Kālī was worshipped as Pūrṇeśvarī in the eastern regions (*pūrvāmnāya*), Viśveśvarī in the southern region (*dakṣiṇā-mnāya*), Kubjikā in the Western region (*paścimāmnāya*), Kālī in the northern region (*uttarāmnāya*), and as Śrīvidyā in the upper region (*ūrdhvāmnāya*). The *Parātantra* describes her in some detail (Paṭalas 2 to 4).

Besides these forms in which Goddesss Kālī is said to be worshipped in different regions according to the *Parātantra*, mention may be made of other forms of Kālī in which she is worshipped by her devotees. These are Dakṣiṇa Kālī, Vāmā Kālī, Śmaśāna Kālī, Kāla Kālī, Kāma Kālī, Bhadra Kālī, Kalasaṁkirśaṇī Kālī, etc. The worship of Dakṣiṇa Kālī is very popular in the eastern part of the country. It is well-known that great spiritual *sādhakas* like Sarvānanda, Śrī Rāmakṛṣṇa Paramahaṁsa or Rāmaprasāda Sen were very ardent devotees of Goddess Dakṣiṇa Kālī.

The different forms of Goddess Kālī in which she is worshipped today are based on the particular form revealed to her devotees during meditation or in dream. For instance, Goddess Kālī appeared in a dream before Rānī Rāsmanī as the 'Saviour of the afflicted', in the world so she got built a temple at Dakṣiṇeśvar dedicated to the worship of Bhavatāriṇī (Kālī) where Śrī Rāmakṛṣṇa was the chief priest.

The vision of Goddess Kālī in concrete form as seen by her devotees is highly symbolic, in the sense that each component, each limb of the Goddess symbolises deep spiritual truths which have been beautifully explained by Mahāmahopādhyāya Gopināth Kavirāj. These may be summarised in the following lines.

Goddess Kālī is visualised by her devotees as standing on a corpse, which is said to be that of Lord Śiva. It is said that when the consciousness force (*caitanya śakti*) functioning remaining confined within the physical framework of Lord Śiva comes out of her free will and starts functioning somewhat separately from Śiva, this results in his assuming the form of a corpse as it were, thereby providing the consciousness force with a suitable locus for her divine play. Goddess Kālī is depicted as having four hands in which she displays two hand postures (*mudrās*) in two hands and holds two weapons in the remaining two. The two right hand postures (*mudrās*) show respectively the Mother Goddess as bestowing boon (*varamudrā*) and giving assurance for protection (*abhayamudrā*) to her devotees. She is depicted as holding a *khaḍga* (scythe) in the upper left hand and the severed head of a demon in the lower left hand. The *khaḍga* symbolises the instrument for cutting asunder or piercing the veil of ignorance covering the intellect of her devotees. The severed head that the goddess is shown holding in one hand represents the *mahāmoha* of Ignorance (*āsurī śakti*) opposed to the divine Śakti in the form of knowledge, and which prevailed before the advent of the goddess. Goddess Kālī is depicted as wearing a garland of severed heads, fifty-two in number, which represent the fifty-two letters of the alphabet of the *devanāgarī* script symbolising the thought-constructs (*vikalpas*) dominating the limited intellect of her devotees. These need to be got rid off before the devotees can obtain a vision of their consciousness nature. The goddess is depicted devoid of dress as she is said to be enwrapped by all pervading ether (*ākāśa*), which has no form or colour. This description of Goddess Kālī (*Dakṣiṇa Kālī*) is given in the *Kālī Tantra*.

Light on her real nature and the mode of worship by her devotees is shed on the *Mahā Kāla Saṁhitā*, a voluminous text now available only in parts, *Kālī Kulārcana* (by Vimalabodha), *Kālīyāmala, Kālī Kalpa, Śyāmārahasya* (by Pūrṇānanda), *Kālīvilāsa Tantra, Kālītantra, Viśvasāra Tantra, Kāmeśvarī Tantra, Kulacuḍāmaṇi Tantra, Kaulāvali, Kulārṇava, Kubjikātantra*, etc.

ii) Goddess Tārā

Goddess Tārā is the only one goddess who is venerated not only in the Hindu tradition but also in the Buddhist Tāntrika tradition by a large number of devotees in this country as also abroad.

In modern times, the worship of the goddess Tārā has been made popular by Vāma Deva of Tārāpiṭha (Birbhum Dist., West Bengal) popularly called Vāmā Kṣepā and his disciple Nigamānanda. Sage Vaśiṣṭha is said to have been an ardent devotee of goddess Tārā in the ancient past.

According to ancient tradition, goddess Tārā is said to symbolise the *Parāvak* in embodied form. She is held to be of the nature of *Pūrṇāhaṁtā* (the pure 'I experience' in absolute form).

Light on her real nature and the mode of worship by her devotees has been shed in *Tārātantra*, *Tārāsūkta, Toḍala Tantra, Tārārṇava, Nīlatantra*, *Mahānīlatantra*, *Cinācāratantra, Tārāsadbhava Tantra, Tāropaniṣad*, etc. Besides these, *Tārābhaktisudhārṇava* by Narasinha Thakkaur, *Tārārahasya* by Śaṅkara, *Tārābhakti Taraṅgiṇī* by Prakaśānanda, *Tārābhakti-taraṅginī* by Vimalānanda, etc are popular texts.

iii) Goddess Ṣoḍaśī

The very name Ṣoḍaśī is indicative of the fullness-nature of the Goddess, on the analogy of the full moon shinning in the firmament and dispelling darkness on a full-moon day. The physical moon is believed to comprise 15 digits, which go on adding one by one with the passage of lunar *tithis* in the bright fortnight, but as sixteen digits constitute the very being of Goddess Ṣoḍaśī, this symbolises that her fullness is more than that of the full moon. As a matter of fact, her nature has been conceptualised as *turīya*, the Transcendent one. As such, She is said to be incapable of being grasped by any instrument of knowledge.

Goddess Soḍaśī is also known by the names of Śrīvidyā and Tripurasundarī to her devotees. Among her devotees who are said to have received her grace and who also popularised her worship were

Manmatha or Kāmadeva, Manu, Candra, Kubera, Lopāmudrā, Agastya, Agni, Sūrya, Indra, Skanda, Śiva and Durvāsā, who was also known as Anger personified (*Krodha Bhaṭṭāraka*). Both Agastya and Lopāmudrā were sages belonging to the Vedic tradition but, according to the *Tripurā Rahasya* (*jñānakhaṇḍa* — section on *jñāna*), they developed a leaning towards the Tāntrika tradition after receiving the grace from the Goddess.

The twelve Vidyeśvaras, the legendary propagators of the worship of Śrīvidyā, played a leading role in popularising her worship throughout the entire length and breadth of the country. There were three main centres of her worship located at Kāmagiri on the sea shore in the east, Jālandhāra atop the mount Meru in the north, and Pūrṇagiri along the sea shore in the west — forming a triangle as it were to cover the entire country.

Besides these, the Goddess was said to be worshipped at 12 different places in different forms, e.g. as Kāmākṣī at Kāñcipuram, as Bhrāmarī in the region called Malayagiri, as Kumārī at Kanyākumārī, as Ambā at Anarta in Gujarat, as Mahālakṣmī at Karabīra, as Kālikā in Malwa, as Lalitā at Prayāg. Vindhyavāsinī in Vindhyācala (Uttar Pradesh) as Viśālakṣī at Vārāṇasī, as Maṅgalacandī at Gayā, as Sundarī in Bengal and Gūhyeśvarī in Nepal (vide *Brahmapurāṇa* IV, 3a).

Ādi Śaṅkarācārya was a follower of the Śrīvidyā tradition for his spiritual practices, which is evident from the fact that he installed a *śrīcakra* in all the *maṭhas* that he established. This also fortifies our contention that worship of Śrīvidyā was in the beginning common to both the Vedic and the Tantric traditions.

According to another view, the followers of Śrīvidyā can be broadly classified under three heads, namely the followers of Kādividyā, of Hādividyā and of Kahādividyā. The Kādividyā has some affinity with the Vedic tradition, and it has been kept secret there. It is extremely esoteric in nature, hence its real nature is known only to a chosen few initiates. Śrīvidyā is worshipped by her devotees as Kālī Śrīvidyārṇava, Tripuropaniṣad and the texts belonging to this tradition are the *Kaulopaniṣad*, *Tantrarāja*, *Mātṛkārṇava*, *Yoginīhṛdaya*, etc. The Hādividyā tradition, leaning more on the side of the Tantras, has Durvāsā as its chief propagator. It prevailed in Kashmir. The *Tripuratāpinī Upaniṣad*, *Vāmakeśvara Tantra, Yoginīhṛdaya*, etc are the texts which are said to belong to this tradition according to Bhāskararāya in his *Varivasyārahasya*. The deity worshipped is Tripura Sundarī. The Kahādividyā was popular in the South, especially Kerala. The Goddess of this tradition is Tārā or Nīlasarasvatī. The Tāntrika texts propagating this tradition are *Jñānarṇava*, *Dakṣināmūrti Saṁhitā*, *Svacchanda Tantra*, *Kalottaravāsanā*, *Saụbhāgya Sudhodaya*, *Śakti-Saṅgama Tantra*, etc.

All these sub-schools within Śrīvidyā differ mainly in respect of the mode of worship prescribed by each of them. Śrīvidyā has made a great impact on the religio-philosophical thought that developed later.

iv) Goddess Bhuvaneśvarī

The worship of the Goddess Bhuvaneśvarī remained confined to isolated pockets with a limited number of devotees. *Bhuvaneśvarī Tantra*, *Bhuvaneśvarī Pārijata*, *Bhuvaneśvarī Rahasya* and *Bhuvaneśvarī Stotra* by Pṛthvīdharācārya are the few texts in which the nature of the Goddess and the rituals connected with her worship are described. Pṛthvīdhara is said to have been a disciple of Ādi Śaṅkara, and is said to have been connected with the Śṛṅgeri Maṭha. Probably this tradition prevailed only in the South.

v) Goddess Bhairavī

Goddesss Bhairavī was worshipped by her devotees mainly in the North. Her nature and mode of worship can be known from the *Bhairavī Tantra*, *Bhairavī Rahasya*, *Bhairavī Saparyāsiddhi*, etc. There is a *Yamāla* text bearing her name. Bhairavī was worshipped in different forms, such as Siddhibhairavī, Tripurā Bhairavī, Caitanya Bhairavī, Kameśvarī Bhairavī, Nityā Bhairavī, etc.

vi) Goddess Chinnamastā

Goddess Chinnamastā has a terrible form, hence she has very few devotees. Also, the mode of worship of this Goddess is very difficult to follow. The *Śaktisaṅgama Tantra* in its section named *Chinnamastā* throws some light on her nature.

vii) Goddess Dhūmāvatī

Goddess Dhūmāvatī is the deity belonging to the northern region (*uttarāmnāya*). She is represented wearing a white dress and holding a winnowing instrument in one of her hands. She is depicted as an emaciated witch-like goddess. She is invoked by her devotees for vanquishing their enemies. Her nature has been described in the *Prāṇatoṣiṇī Tantra*.

viii) Goddess Bagalā

Goddess Bagalā is invoked for paralysing the activities of enemies in all the three spheres of creation. The *Sāṅkhyāyana Tantra*, *Bagalā Karma Kalpāvallī* describe her exploits in *Satyayuga*, when Viṣṇu is said to have invoked her help to tide over a natural upheaval. Datia in Madhya Pradesh is well-known for sheltering a temple dedicated to her worship.

ix) Goddess Mātaṅgī

Goddess Mātaṅgī is depicted as having a fierce look. According to *Brahmayāmala*, the Goddess, pleased with the austerities performed by sage Mataṅga, incarnated in the family of the sage as his daughter; therefore she bears the name Mātaṅgī. The *Mātaṅgī Krama* and *Mātaṅgī Paddhati* are two well-known texts shedding light on her nature and mode of worship.

x) Goddess Kamalā

Goddess Kamalā is a very adorable Goddess on account of her fair complexion and charming face. She is bedecked with garlands made from priceless gems and wears a beautiful crown on her head.

Four white elephants from the snowclad Himalayan peaks are depicted as continuously pouring holy waters from four golden jars which they hold with their trunks. She sits on a beautiful lotus. The *Śaradātilaka*, *Śāktapramoda* and *Tantrasāra* of Kṛṣṇānanda Āgamavagiśa describe her form and mode of worship.

Besides these, the Kaula School was a very powerful Śākta school, which held to sway not only in the Himalaya region but also in the South. The origin of the Kaula School of thought can be traditionally traced back to Bhairavī (a form of goddess Pārvatī), who passed on the spiritual wisdom to Svacchanda Bhairava. It was later passed on to Matsyendranātha, also known as Lui Pa in the Tibetan tradition. It is said that he was head of the Kāmarūpa Pīṭha; later he emerged as a prominent exponent of Kūlamārga. His disciple Śambhunātha was a famous *siddha* belonging to the lineage of Kaula teachers. He lived in Jālandhara Pītha. He was well known as the teacher of Abhinavagupta, who paid obeisance to him in his *Tantrāloka*.[96]

The Kaula school of thought possessed a very rich literature; it exerted a great influence on the Trika School of Kāśmira, but later got merged in it due to the great affinity existing between these two schools. Among the books which describe the metaphysical tenets of this school, mention may be made of the *Kulārṇava, Kulacūḍāmaṇi, Rudrayāmala, Devīyāmala, Kulapañcāmṛta, Uttaratantra, Kulatantra, Tantra Cūḍāmaṇi, Kulakamala, Kulapradīpa, Marutantra, Kula Sarvasva, Kula Sāra, Kaula Tantra, Kaulādarśa Tantra, Kularahasya, Rahasyārṇava, Śrītattva Cintāmaṇi, Śāmbhavī Tantra, Gandharva Tantra, Vāmakeśvara, Tantrarāja Āgama, Sara, Kaulopaniṣad, Guhyopaniṣad, Paraśurāma Kalpa-sūtra*,[97] etc. All these texts are not available. Not only Kaulas themselves but also the Kashmirian *ācārya* Kṣemarāja in his commentary on the

---

[96] *Ibid*, p. 115 and 178.

[97] Dr. G.N. Kaviraj has given a long list of the works belonging to this school of thought in p. 37.

Vijñānabhairava Tantra[98] has praised Kaula Siddhānta. However, Lakṣmīdhara in his commentary on *Saundarya Laharī* condemned the Kaula philosophy as being anti-Vedic, and therefore not acceptable to him.

For centuries, the Tantric texts and practices remained confined within a narrow group of spiritual practitioners who had been initiated into the secret lore of the Tantras. This resulted in Tantric practices being confined within initiated groups of practitioners; they did not gain currency among the masses. In fact, most of the Tantric texts end up with the instruction that their practices should not be revealed to other than initiated practitioners (*sarvathā gopyam*), lest these could be misused by unscrupulous *sādhakas* and misunderstood by lay people. The secrecy observed by *sādhakas* caused, on one hand, the development of a general feeling of abhorrence and antipathy towards Tantras and Tantric practices, and on the other hand, the disappearance of a vast literature and the gradual drying up of the Tantric tradition. But it must be admitted in fairness that, though the Tantric tradition has disappeared from the scene, it has percolated into the routine religious practices that devout Hindus perform in their daily life even today.

The Kaulas preferred following the *vāmācāra* (left hand practices) as against the *dakṣinācāra* (right hand practices) followed by the practitioners of the Śrīvidyā tradition. The *vāmācāra* became very popular with the Śākta spiritual practitioners in Bengal, Assam and Nepal. As to the question of who is a Kaula, it is stated in the *Svacchanda Tantra* that *kula* signifies Śakti, i.e. *Kuṇḍalinī Śakti*, while *akula* means Śiva. The objective of Kaula Śākta practitioners is to achieve the union of *kula* with *akula*, Śakti with Śiva, which are said to be located in the *Mulādhāra* and the *Sahasrāra cakras* respectively.

[98] *Op. Cit.*, p. 4.

There is a great deal of misconception about the spiritual practices followed by left-handed Śākta practitioners. This is due to the secrecy observed by the followers of this mode of spiritual discipline, technically called *pañca-makāra sādhanā* (the five practices bearing a name beginning with *ma*). Very few people know that all the five modes of spiritual discipline included in *pañca-makāra* are symbolic in nature. Outwardly they might appear to be nauseating practices for which their condemnation appears to be fully justified, but they have an inner meaning which is revealed to the initiated few by the spiritual teacher (*guru*) who trains them in the proper way. The *pañcamakāra* practices have been enumerated in this way.

The five *makāras* are *madya* (lit. drinking of wine), *māṁsa* (eating meat), *mīna* (taking of fish), *mudrā* (showing of certain hand postures) and *maithuna* (copulation).

The *Kulārṇava Tantra* and the *Viśvasāra Tantra* reveal their inner meaning one by one, shedding light on their significance in spiritual terms. For instance, the *Kulārṇava Tantra* tells us that the term *madya* does not signify wine, but rather means the nectar which is said to ooze drop by drop from the thousand-petalled lotus situated in the crown of the *sādhaka*. He is enjoined by the Tantra to drink this nectar coming down within him during the performance of his spiritual practices and become intoxicated with delight during the practice of *Kuṇḍalinī Yoga*.

The *Gandharva Tantra* says the same thing in its own way. It tells us that the *yogin* should taste the real nectar falling drop by drop from the junction of the palate with the tongue. This is totally different from that which is produced from the fermentation of jaggery.

The term *māṁsa* does not signify the meat in gross form, for the *Kulārṇava Tantra* says that, "that real *sādhaka* is said to be a devourer of meat who, after 'killing' the 'animal' in him in the form of piety and the sin by the sword of knowledge, succeeds in 'dissolving his mind', the repository of all mundane thoughts, in the Supreme Being."

The term 'fish' is symbolised by the incoming and outgoing breaths. The *Āgama Sāra Tantra* says — two 'fishes' in the form of inhalation and exhalation of breath constantly move upward and downward through the two nerve channels, *īḍā* and *piṅgalā*, represented by the two rivers Gaṅgā and Yamunā, existing within the gross physical body of all embodied beings. The *yogins* should 'eat' them; that is described as the *sādhaka* well-versed in the act of stopping them altogether. Such *sādhaka* succeeds in stopping the passage of time within him.

The term *mudrā* literally means showing certain postures of the hands, which gladden the 'deity'. In the context of the Tantric *sādhanā*, *mudrā* signifies the giving up of the company of evil persons. The *Vijaya Tantra* explains the meaning of *mudrā* as avoiding the company of evil persons who corrupt the intellect. This is because the company of sinful persons leads one to bondage, while association with pious persons is conducive to the achievement of liberation.

The term *maithuna* (lit. sexual intercourse) actually connotes joining together. In the context of *sādhanā*, the joining or uniting the *Kuṇḍalini Śakti* with Śiva, located respectively in the *mūlādhāra cakra* and the *sahasrāra* in the gross physical body of all *sādhakas*, is *maithuna*. It results in the fusion of Śakti, representing the dynamic aspect, with Śiva, symbolising the static aspect, who are separated due to the self-imposed self-contraction (*sañkoca*) at the time of creation on the mundane level. It is clear from this that *maithuna* in the context of *sādhanā* does not signify copulation in a gross physical sense.

Thus the *pañca makāra* practices prescribed by some Śākta schools is not the obnoxious practice for which the Tantras are maligned by ignorant people. It has an inner meaning, which is revealed by the *guru* to the *sādhaka* initiated by him after testing his fitness and strength of character. It is kept secret to all others who lack fitness and capacity to control their senses. They are prohibited from following this hazardous path, a path which is "like treading on a sharp-edged sword", that all cannot undertake.

~CHAPTER II~

Salient Features
of the Language of the Tantras

The Tantras are traditionally held to have emanated from the different faces of the Supreme Lord, Śiva.[1] They are, therefore, classed under the category of revealed texts.[2] As revealed texts, they embody certain characteristics commonly found in all revealed scriptures of the world, viz the *Vedas*, the *Upaniṣads*, the *Bible*, the Holy *Quran*, etc. Some of these characteristics are — predominance of an esoteric element, description of superhuman powers, a mystic element, use of symbolic language, etc. The Tantras too possess these characteristics in abundant measure.

Though most of the Tantras are found to have been written in the form of a conversation between Lord Śiva and his consort Pārvatī, or the Teacher and his disciple, in classical Sanskrit language, the use of symbolic imagery and language very often creates difficulty in our understanding the true significance of the texts. The description of occult practices in which symbolic *mantras* occur very frequently is not always intelligible, owing to our not knowing the secret code in which it is expressed. In fact, even if we are somehow able to decipher its apparent meaning, the words used there to convey the secret tradition (*rahasya vidyā*)[3] appear to signify multiple meanings, one obvious and the other meaning remaining hidden, a mystery.

---

[1] The five faces are Iśāna, Tatpuruṣa, Sadyojāta, Aghora, and Vāmadeva, which respectively are said to represent the five aspects (*cit, ānanda, icchā, jñāna*, and *kriyā*) of the Supreme Lord's divine essence.

[2] For the divine origin of Śaiva Tantras, see MVT, Introduction.

[3] Cf. Śiv. Dr. VII 107-113.

It may be asked why Tantras employ such language when all other contemporaneous philosophical texts speak in plain terms, yielding only one meaning to all. The reason is not far to seek. The Tantras in general deal with intuitive religious experiences of the adepts or the occult practices prescribed for obtaining such religious experiences. These intuitive experiences are far too deep and full of great significance, and cannot be adequately conveyed by our ordinary language. Hence the symbolic language had to be employed to bring out the depth of meaning, as it is the only language that has multi-dimensional significance, and therefore possesses the capacity to reveal the inner significance, the totality of meaning.

In her book *Mysticism*, Underhill has rightly observed, "The mystic, as a rule, cannot wholly do without symbol and image, as ordinary language is inadequate to his vision. He feels that his experience must be expressed. If it is to be communicated, and it actually is inexpressible except in some sidelong way, some hint or parallel has to be given which would stimulate the dormant intuition of the readers, and convey as all poetic language does, some thing beyond the surface sense."[4] This applies fully to the Tāntrika texts, which abound in esoteric content.

The symbolic language is very often a 'clothed' language, not literal but suggestive, discernable only to those who have been initiated to the secret lore. Tucci in his book *Tibetan Painted Scrolls* (Rome, 1949)[5] has rightly pointed out the distinction between 'literal' and 'allegorical' meaning as is found in the *Guhyasamāja Tantra*, a Buddhist Tantra. Lama Anāgarika Govinda has spoken of the 'twilight language' (*saṁdhyā bhāṣā*) employed by the Tantras, which is said to bear a double meaning, the ordinary and the mystic.[6] The ordinary meaning is the literal one, while the mystic meaning is the inner secret one, which forms the kernel of the Tantras. Mircea Eliade in his book

---

[4] E. Underhill, *Mysticism*, London, 1956, p. 79.

[5] *Op. cit.*, p. 7 ff. n. 13.

[6] *Foundations of Tibetan Mysticism*, New York, 1960, p. 53.

Yoga, Immortality and Freedom[7] has thrown light on the necessity for using 'twilight' language in the Tantras. According to him, the preservation of the secrecy of Tantric doctrines and occult practices and the prevention of its misuse by unscrupulous non-initiates are the principal motives which impelled the Tāntrikas to use such language, which conveys one meaning to the lay people and another, more pregnant one, to the followers of the tradition.

A few illustrations from the Tantras would clarify this point. The *Mālinīvijayottara Tantra* [8] refers to five different kinds of intuitive experience, which an aspirant has at every step of his ascent from the material level to the spiritual levels. These are *ānanda, udbhava, kampa, nidrā, ghūrṇi*.[9] If we take the literal meaning of these five terms, these hardly signify something worthwhile, and, in that case, we fail to grasp the real import which is essentially esoteric and spiritual. For instance, the term *ānanda* here does not simply mean delight, but delight of a particular kind. In fact all these spiritual experiences are indicative of the aspirant's firm establishment in a particular level of ascent, as also of his release in gradual stages from the clutches of matter. As the aspirant steps on a particular stage of ascent, he experiences Delight, which is due to two factors. Firstly, as he enters a particular step, he establishes contact (*sparśa*), as it were, with his pure self. The 'touch' of the pure self fills him with a unique kind of spiritual delight. Secondly, his rise to a particular level of existence marks the beginning of the 'dissolution' of his intricate connection with matter.[10]

The experience of 'melting away' this intimate relationship grows in gradual steps till the aspirant finally feels himself completely dissociated from matter. As a result of this, he feels himself disembodied as it were. This leads to his experiencing a peculiar feeling

---

[7] Published from Princeton, 1958 pp. 249-54.

[8] Published in the Kāśmīra Series of Texts and Studies, Srinagar.

[9] *Mālinīvijaya Vārttika* II. 38 ff.

[10] For details, see the author's article: 'Esoteric Elements in the Trika Philosophy of Kāśmīr' in *Kuruksetra University Research Journal*, Vol. VI No. 2, 1972, pp. 197-206.

of buoyancy and rising up which has technically been called *udbhava* or upward motion.

In this connection it may be pointed out here that the association of spirit with matter is on such a complex scale that their complete dissociation is a long-drawn process, and it is, in fact, achieved by the *sādhaka* only after his attaining divine union (*samāveśa*). In this stage, he merely succeeds in untying, as it were, one of the several knots (*granthi*)[11] of this association, which causes this feeling of buoyancy in him.

With the slight slackening of the intimate relation of the self with the not-self in every step of his ascent, a kind of self-consciousness or awareness (*ātmabhāvanā*) grows in the aspirant, and he now turns his attention more and more towards his real self. As a result of this, his physical body, which was receiving most of his attention previously, becomes deprived of all support, and it begins shaking as it were, before it completely disappears from his view. This particular experience is technically called *kampa* or 'shaking'.

With the disappearance of the material body from his 'gaze' he is left with nothing to experience. As a consequence of this, he feels overtaken by a sleep-like quiescence and peace. This unique experience of peace and the consequent cessation of movements of all his sense organs — internal as well external — is called *nidrā* or 'sleep'.

When the aspirant reaches that state in which he experiences the dissolution of the sense of identity of spirit with matter, consequent on the disappearance of the material body from his 'gaze' as it were, this vision of his real self makes him realise that It alone is, and that there is nothing apart from his self. He looks around him to find that the entire universe is only his own self-manifestation. This experience, consequent on his looking round himself, is technically called *ghūrṇi*.[12]

---

[11] Cf. *bhidyate hṛdaya granthi chidyate sarva saṁśayāh, tasmin dṛṣṭe parāvare* | *Muṇḍakopaniṣat* II, 2,8.

[12] Cf Author's article 'Esoteric Elements in the Trika Philosophy of Kāśmira' in the *Kurukshetra Univ. Research Journal* VI, No.2, 1972, pp. 197-205. 126700.

As the aspirant has all these mystic experiences in a particular level of hs spiritual ascent, he is said to accomplish a firm establishment in that particular step (*viśrānti*), and thus qualify for further ascent to higher stages. It may be mentioned here that the *Mālinīvijayottara Tantra* does not give detailed explanations of mystic experiences as given above. We have to look for the hidden meaning in the Tantric tradition where the true significance of these experiences is preserved.

We would like to give another example from the Śākta Tantras to illustrate our contention. The Kaulas form an important branch of the Śākta tradition, and certain Śākta Tantras belonging to the Kaula stream have defined a Kaula *sādhaka* and explained his mode of spiritual discipline, technically called *Kulācāra*.[13] According to the *Svacchanda Tantra*, a Kaula is not a person born in a *kula*, i.e. a family, but one who is capable of uniting *Kula*, i.e. the Serpent Power (*Kundalinī Śakti*), with *Akula*, i.e., Śiva stationed on the *sahasrāra cakra*, by arousing the former and effecting its ascent through the five *cakras* (plexuses).[14] The *Kulācara* thus does not denote certain family rites but the performance of a particular kind of spiritual discipline consisting of the five '*makāras*' that have been enumerated in the *Kulārṇava Tantra* as *madya* (wine), *māṁsa* (flesh), *matsya* (fish), *mudrā* and *maithuna* (sexual intercourse).[15] These five *makāras* too have a double connotation, one gross based on the literal meaning and the hidden one belonging to the spiritual field. If we take the literal meaning of these five *makāras* or aspects of spiritual discipline, they denote certain rites and practices which are definitely obscene and disgusting. The hidden meaning symbolises certain rites

---

[13] For desciption of *kuladharma* and *kulācāra*, see *Kulārṇava Tantra*, Ullāsa II.

[14] *Kulam, śaktiriti proktam kulam śiva ucyate | Kule, kulasya sambandhaḥ kaula nittiyabhidhīyate || Svaccha. Tantra*. Advaita Śaiva writers give as many meanings of the term *kaula* in the *Pārātriṁśikā Vivaraṇa*.

[15] *Madyani māṁsyānī ca mīncṁ ca mudrā maithunameva ca | makārapañcakam prāhuryoginām muktidāyakam || Kulārṇava Tantra*. Also compare *Mahānirvāṇa Tantra* I, 59 P. 13 (Jivānanda Vidyāsāgara Ed. 1884). See also Chapter One in this work.

which an aspirant, following the Śākta Tāntrika mode of discipline, is required to perform within himself after receiving initiation and the appropriate training from a *guru*. For example, the term *madya* (lit. wine) does not stand for the intoxicant wine but the divine nectar that is said ooze from the thousand-petalled lotus in the *brahmarandhra*. The drinking of this nectar after one has secured ascent to a higher spiritual level by performing *khecarī mudrā* is said to fill the aspirant with Divine Delight.[16]

Likewise, *māṁsa* (flesh) does not signify the physical flesh which the aspirant should eat. Flesh, in this context, means the flesh of the 'beast' (*paśu*) in him, which must be destroyed. It has been enjoined that the aspirant should kill the 'beast' in him, constituted by merit and demerit with the blade of the sword of knowledge (*jnāna-khaḍga*) and devour its flesh.[17] The taking of flesh thus is tantamount to getting rid of beastliness in man.

Matsya literally means fish, but, in this context, it symbolically signifies the inhalation and exhalation of breath (*prāṇāpaṇa*). It has been said that the two *nāḍīs*, *iḍā* and *piṅgalā*, which are also named as *Gaṅgā* and *Yamunā*, have two fishes, viz inhalation and exhalation, moving constantly up and down. It is enjoined that a follower of the Śākta mode of spiritual discipline should stop their erratic movements by performing *kumbhaka* (stopping of breath) through *prāṇāyāma* (control of breath)[18] so that the blocked channel of the central *nāḍī*, viz *suṣumnā*, could be opened for the ascent of *kuṇḍalinī śakti*. This is symbolically called the 'eating of fish' (*matsya bhakṣaṇa*), and the aspirants who practice it are known as *matsya-sādhaka*.

Mudrā literally means positioning the fingers in a prescribed posture, but in the context of Tantric *sādhanā* it signifies the giving

---

[16] *Vyomā paṅkajam nisyandasudhāpāna-rato naraḥ; madhupāyī samaḥ proktasvitare madyapāyinaḥ* | II, *Kulārṇava Tantra* V. 108.

[17] *Puṇyāpuṇya paśuṁ hatvā jñānakhaḍgena yogact/para layaṁ nayeccittam maṁsāsi sa nigadyate* | 11, Ibid, 109.

[18] Cf. *Gaṅgāyamunāyormadhye dvau matsan carataḥ sadā* | *tau matsyān bhakṣayet yastu sa bhavenmatsya sādhakā* || Also see *Kulārṇava Tantra* V, 110. *Āgamasāra*.

up of bad company. The *Vijaya Tantra* says that the company of the virtuous (*satsaṅga*) leads the aspirant to liberation, while bad company causes bondage. The achievement of the severance by the *sādhaka* of his relationship with bad people is *mudrā*.[19]

Maithuna literally means 'sexual intercourse' but in the Śākta tradition of *sādhana*, it symbolically signifies the union of *kuṇḍalinī śakti* (serpent power) with Śiva, who rests on the *sahasrāra cakra*. It has been enjoined that the aspirant should direct the vital breath through the *suṣumnā nāḍī* after controlling its movement in the two *nāḍīs*, viz *iḍā* and *piṅgalā*, that lie parallel to the *suṣumnā*, and thereby effect the union. The union of these two leads the aspirant to experience an ecstatic delight which has no parallel in the physical world.[20]

Thus we find that there exists a big gap between the literal and the symbolic meanings of the words used in the Tantras, especially to describe the Tantric mode of spiritual discipline. This big gap in the two meanings cannot be bridged without taking recourse to the oral Tāntrika tradition in which secret meanings are transmitted from the master to his initiated disciple, who alone is considered fit to receive instructions in the secret lore. In fact, because of our ignorance of the true significance of symbolic mystic expressions in Tantric texts, the Tantric rites and practices have not only been misunderstood but also very much abused by unscrupulous persons, for the Tāntrika tradition, by its very nature, is not an open tradition. It is available to only a select few who are considered to be *adhikārins* (qualified persons) for receiving instructions for performing spiritual practices.[21]

---

[19] *Satsaṅgena bhavenmukti-rasatsaṅgesu bandhana | asatsaṅgamudrāṇām yattu tanmudrā parikīrtitā* || Ibid.

[20] Cf. *iḍāpingalayoh prāṇān suṣumnāyam pravartayet | suṣumṇā śaktiruddiṣṭā jīvo, yam tu paraḥ śivaḥ || tayotsaṅgame devaiḥ suratam̐ nāma kīrtitam* | Also see *Kulārṇava Tantra*, V, 112.

[21] Cf. *Mahānirvāṇa Tantra* II, 22, p. 19 (Jīvānanda Vidyāsāgara ed.).

~Chapter III~

The Supreme Reality in the Śaiva Tantras

Every school of yoga has its own metaphysical system, and the Tantras are no exception to this general trend. There are several currents in the Tantric stream, such as *dvaita* (dualistic), *dvaitādvaita* (dualistic-cum-monistic) and *advaita* (monistic), besides the broad currents of the Vaiṣṇava, Śaiva and Śākta, each postulating its own scheme of philosophy and prescribing its distinct modes of spiritual discipline (*sādhanakriyā*). In order to grasp the true significance of Tantra-Yoga, it is essential to know the metaphysical background propagated by a particular Tantric tradition. The ultimate destiny and the starting point in the spiritual journey to the Supreme Goal must first be spelled out before the study of Tantra-Yoga can be undertaken. The nature of man and his position in creation must also be ascertained for the simple reason that the system of yoga has been prescribed for him only.

The ultimate destiny, according to the Śaiva Tantras, especially those prevalent in Kashmir, is the recognition of one's Śiva-nature (*Śivatva*),[1] for He is said to be the Supreme Reality. He has also been called *Pati*, the Lord, in the Śaiva Tantras.

Man is only a self-limited form of the highest reality *Parama Śiva*,[2] and, on account of his being enwrapped by various bonds or *pāśas*, he is given the name of *paśu*. We propose here to discuss the nature of the Supreme Reality as well as that of man in the following paragraphs.

---

1 *Tantrasāra*, Ah II, p. 9.

2 *Mālinīvijaya Vārtika*, v. 69, p. 8.

Parasaṁvid as the Supreme Reality

The Śaiva Tantras, especially those which were prevalent in Kashmir, advocate a purely monistic philosophy.[3] They, therefore, conceive the Supreme Reality as the supreme Experiencing Principle (*Parāsaṁvid*), which is of the nature of pure *caitanya* (consciousness).[4] By its very nature, It is eternal, immutable and infinite. Though it is eternal and immutable, it underlies everything in the universe as the innermost and true self,[5] both individually and collectively. That is to say, it pervades and permeates the entire cosmos.[6] At the same time, It is not exhausted by its innumerable and diverse manifestations as universe, nor is limited by space (*deśa*), time (*kāla*), and form (*rūpa*). It transcends all and is beyond all, and hence, in that transcending aspect,[7] it is given the name *Tattvātīta* or *Anuttara* (Absolute).

The *Parāsaṁvid*, thus, has a two-fold nature: as the underlying Reality of everything, It is the all-pervasive and all-inclusive cosmic Reality, the Universal *caitanya* (*viśvātmaka caitanya*); and, at the same time, It is also the all-transcending (*viśvottīrṇa*) Supreme Reality, the Absolute Being.[8] It has been variously designated as the *Parācit*, *Anuttara*, *Parameśvara*, *Parama Śiva*.[9]

The Supreme Reality *Parama Śiva* is said to be endowed with *Śakti*, which actually is identical with His essence.[10] *Śakti* in fact represents the dynamic side of His nature, whereby He is said to be ever active and always revealing Himself to Himself in the absence of a second.[11] His possession of *Śakti* as an integral aspect of His nature is indicative of His Fullness (*pūrṇatva*) and Absolute character.[12]

---

3 *Malinīvijayottara Tantra*, *Svacchanda Tantra*, *Mṛgendra Tantra*, *Netra Tantra*, etc, popular mainly in Kashmir, advocate monism, though some of them were interpreted differently before the advent of *ācāryas* like Vasugupta, Somānanda, Abhinavagupta, Kṣemarāja, etc.

4 Śiv Sū Sū 1.

5 *Ibid*.

6 *Vijñānabhairava Tantra* v. 132.

7 Cf. *Mālinīvijaya Vārtika* II, 126; *Parātriṁśika* ix. p. 19.

8 *Ibid*. I, v. 124-26.

9 *Ibid* I. v. 69; *Vijñānabhairava* v. 57 cm.

10 *Vijñānabhairava* v. 18.

11 *Ibid*, v. 21.

12 *Ibid*, v. 20.

His Śakti is absolutely free from any kind of restriction or limitation, and is, therefore, technically called *svātantrya śakti* (Divine Freedom).[13] His Divine Freedom consists in His forming Divine Resolve (*saṅkalpa*), and then translating them in actuality through His Power of Action (*kriyā*).[14] He thus possesses not only an unlimited Freedom of will (*icchā*) of forming Divine Resolves but also an absolute freedom of carrying them out, i.e. Freedom of Action (*kriyā*), which together constitute the essence of His divinity (*pārameśvarya*).

Exercising His divine freedom (*svātantrya*), the Supreme Lord or Parama Śiva, sometimes, i.e. during the period of creative activity, reveals Himself to Himself in the absence of a second as the universe (*viśva*).[15] Of this, the self-revelation as universe, which He does out of His free and independent will (*svechayā*)[16] with Himself as the substratum or background (*bhitti*), He is the Agent (*kartā*), the Experience (*jñātā*) and the Enjoyer (*bhoktā*). The manifestation of the universe is thus only a mode of His self-revelation (*svaprakāśa*) in which He utilises no other material except His own Śakti, the *Svātantrya Śakti*.

Or to put it in the technical language of the Tantras, Parama Śiva's self-manifestation as the universe is only a self-expansion in the aspect of His divine Śakti (*svaśakti-sphāra*).[17] As such, the manifestation of the universe symbolises His divine Glory (*aiśvasrya*) in the revelation of which the Śakti plays a pivotal role.

Divine Śakti, her nature and role in the manifestation of the universe

The divine Śakti is said to be ever active and therefore always revealing His divine Glory.[18] There are two ways in which the divine Śakti functions and brings out the divine Glory of the Supreme Lord. When the divine Śakti functions as identified with Him, it reveals

[13] *Vijñānabhairava*, v. 82.

[14] *Ibid*, v. 57.

[15] Cf. *Svacchanda Tantra* II, 295 Comm.

[16] Cf. MVT I, 18.

[17] *Śiv. Sū*. I, 6, Comm p. 21.

[18] *Ibid*, I, 5 Comm. pp. 18-9.

His divine Glory (*aiśvarya*) in the form of self-experience as *pūrṇāhamtā*. On the other hand, when it functions somewhat differently (*bhedena*), it is responsible for bringing about the revelation of the universe which was till then lying absorbed in and identified with the Essence of the Supreme Lord. Śakti has therefore been sometimes described as the essence of His divinity, the 'heart' (*hṛdaya*) of the Supreme Lord.[19] It has, therefore, been said that when the Supreme Lord, inseparably fused with His Śakti, opens himself out (*unmiṣati*), the universe comes to be, and when he closes himself up (*nimiṣati*), the universe disappears as a manifestation predicable in terms of discursive thought and speech (*vācya vācaka*).[20] The divine Śakti does this eternally, alternating between a phase of manifestation when the universe comes into existence and a phase of potentiality when the universe assumes a seminal form (*bījāvastha*) as it were, thus revealing the divine Glory of the Supreme Lord both as the universe and as the transcendent Absolute.[21]

The phase of manifestation of Śakti as universe, or, to put it in the technical language of the Tantras, the self-manifestation of the Supreme Lord in the aspect of universe, is *unmeṣa* (opening out), while His self-manifestation as the Supreme Lord has been named as *nimeṣa* or *pralaya*, and the complete cycle of *unmeṣa* and *nimeṣa*[22] as *kalpa* (lit, imagining of creation and its dissolution).

Looking from the point of view of the Supreme Lord, the entire process of self-manifestation as universe can be described as His involution, the descent of the highest Spiritual Principle into diverse forms of matter. Here it must be remembered that when He manifests Himself as the cosmos, He does not undergo any change or suffer any blemish. He remains as He ever is, the immutable transcendent Absolute, the Supreme Lord.[23]

---

[19] Tan. Sār. IV p. 27.

[20] Cf. S.D. 79 ff p. 178; T.A. III.

[21] TA Comm. p. 121.

[22] Cf. I PV III, 1, 3 Com. p. 221-2 (Bhāskārī ed.).

[23] Cf. Pr, Hd. Sū II.

Here it may be pointed out that though the Śaiva Tantras speak of the Supreme Reality as the Supreme Lord, Parama Śiva, and describe His various powers and His Divine Glory, etc, they do not thereby mean to anthropomorphize an abstract metaphysical principle, i.e. *Parācit* or *Parāsaṁvid*, for He has been called formless (*nirākāra*). It would perhaps be not out of place here to examine critically the Tantric conception of the Supreme Reality in the light of the conception of the Supreme Reality as *Brahman* in the *Upaniṣads*, both advocating of purely monistic philosophy, for the sake of a better understanding and a critical appreciation of the Tantric view point.

Although both the *Tantras* and *Upaniṣads* agree in describing the Supreme Reality as essentially of the nature of pure *caitanya*, they differ widely in their conception of its nature. While the *Tantras* conceive pure *caitanya* to be endowed with *śakti*, that is held to be identical with it, and whereby *caitanya* is always self-aware and self-revealed, the *Upaniṣads*, as interpreted by Śaṅkara, maintain that the pure *caitanya* is relation-less, inactive pure Existence (*śuddha sat*) and Pure Bliss *(ānanda*) only. The *Upaniṣads* as seen by the Advaita Vedāntins do not admit the existence of Śakti as an aspect of *caitanya*.

Being endowed with *Śakti*, the Supreme Reality, technically called *Parama Śiva* in the Śaiva Tantras, differs fundamentally from the *Brahman* of the *Upaniṣads* in as much as the former has also been described as the Supreme Lord (*Maheśvara*) and the Free Agent (*svatantra-kartā*).[24] As such, He possesses the absolute freedom (*svātantrya*)[25] of making Himself appear as the universe in Himself as the background.

The universe with its infinite variety of objects (*prameyas*), instruments of experience (*karaṇa*) and experiences (*pramātā*), is something different from Himself; it is, in fact, a manifestation of the immanent aspect of the Supreme Lord. It represents a mode of His self-manifestation (*ābhāsa*) as the world resulting from His divine

[24] Cf. Pr. Hd. Sū 2 Com.

[25] I.P.V.V. vol. I, pp. 8-9.

Resolve (*saṅkalpa*) to become the world. Nothing is needed by Him in translating his resolve except his free will (*svecchā*).[26]

The *Upaniṣads* as interpreted by the Advaita Vedāntins, on the other hand, regard the Supreme Reality, *Brahman*, to be transcendent pure Being (*śuddha sat*) ever-immersed in its essential Nature (*svarūpa*). As such, *Brahman* is absolutely inactive in Itself. Though it is also stated to be the underlying Reality of every appearance, It is in itself one (*ekam*) and indivisible pure Existence (*akhaṇḍa sat*). It has no relation whatsoever with the appearance of the universe, with multiplicity.

The transient world with all its infinite variety appears in *Brahman* due to ignorance (*ajñāna*). Though, being the sole Reality, *Brahman* is the locus or substratum of all appearances and experiences, It is in no way connected with the appearance or perverted experience, as It is immutable and essentially inactive.[27]

It is therefore said in the *Upaniṣads* that the appearance of the world is due to the functioning of a *Śakti*, which, though distinct from *Brahman*, is held to be mysteriously subservient to it. This Śakti, technically called *Māyāśakti*, is described as being of the nature of neither 'is' (*asti*), nor 'is not' (*nāsti*) and therefore indescribable (*anirvacanīya*)[28] in logical terms. It functions ceaselessly in *Brahman*, making the multiplicity to appear.

Brahman is thus reduced to an action-less locus (*āśraya*) on which Māyāśakti operates without any beginning. Though the *Upaniṣads*, as seen by Śaṅkara, do not admit the existence of *Śakti* in *Brahman*, yet the existence of *Śakti* has not been denied altogether, for on account of the appearance of multiplicity in the unity of *Brahman*, the operation of *Śakti* has been admitted, though this *śakti* has been held to be material (*jaḍa*) by nature, while the *Tantras* consider *Śakti* to be essentially of the nature of *caitanya*, and therefore divine.[29]

---

[26] Sp. Ka. V.I. pp. 4-5 Comm.; Pr. Hd. Sū 2.

[27] Cf. S.D. II. 21-23.

[28] Ved. Sār p. 10.

[29] For criticism of the Advaita Vedāntā view point, see SD II, 90, p. 59.

The divergence in the conception of the Supreme Reality as postulated by the two monistic schools of thought, viz the *Tantras* and the *Upaniṣads*, appear to stem from the differences in their conception of the nature of *Śakti*. While he *Upaniṣads* as interpreted by the *advaitācāryas* consider *Śakti*, technically called *Māyā Śakti*, to be inert by its very nature, and therefore very different from the Supreme Reality, *Brahman*, which is regarded as spiritual, the *Tantras* regard *Śakti* too to be spiritual in essence, and, as such, an integral aspect of the Supreme Being,[30] *Parama Śiva*.

Thus, by recognising *Śakti* to be an inalienable aspect of *Parama Śiva*, the Śaiva Tantras appear to enlarge, as it were, their conception of the Supreme Reality, which is both the Transcendent Reality (*viśvottīrṇa*), the Absolute, and the Immanent Existence (*viśvātmaka*) as the universe. As compared to this, the Upaniṣadic view, as seen by Śaṅkara, of the Supreme Reality *Brahman* appears to be truncated, narrow and exclusive, based as it were on the negative outlook (*neti neti*).

It has already been observed that *Śakti* is the essence of the Supreme Lord's divinity. Always functioning as identified with Him and thus revealing His divine Glory (*aiśvarya*) sometimes as the Supreme Lord, sometimes as the world, it has innumerable forms or aspects, which however can be subsumed under five principal heads, viz *cit*, *ānanda*, *icchā*, *jñāṇā* and *kriyā*,[31] arranged in order of their intrinsicality.

Cit śakti is the most intrinsic aspect, symbolising the Supreme Lord's power of self-revelation (*prakāśarūpatā*).[32] As she functions as identified with Him, He always shines and reveals Himself to Himself in he absence of a second. This self-revelation, it is said, is of the nature of the 'Being experience' (*Aham*) of the Supreme Lord, and as such is eternal (*nitya*) and 'Full-in-itself' (*pūrṇa*).

Next in order of intrinsicality is the *Ānanda śakti*, due to which the Supreme Lord, who is Full-in-Himself' (*paripūrṇa svabhāva*) feels

---

[30] Cf S.D. II, 28-30 Com. p. 53.

[31] Tan. Sar VIII, p. 73 f.

ever-satisfied (*ātma tṛpta*) and ever at rest. He does not experience any defficiency or want for which He might feel the necessity of moving out of Himself for satisfaction or joy. He remains, as it were, resting always in Himself (*svātmaviśrānta*),[33] immersed in His Essence and experiencing an ever-undisturbed Peace and Bliss.[34]

The *Icchā śakti* is that aspect of the divine Śakti by which the Supreme Lord feels Himself supremely able and possessed of the absolute Will of forming divine Resolve (*saṅkalpa*) as to what to do or what to become (*bubhuṣālakṣana*).[35] The divine Resolve is at the root of all His movements and acts (*kriyā*), including the manifestation of the multiplicity in Himself as the background.[36] This *Icchā śakti* is therefore the most important aspect of the divine Śakti from the point of view of creation (*sṛṣṭi*).

The *Jñāna śakti* is that aspect of the divine Śakti which brings in and holds all his self-manifestations as object (*prameya kalpa*) in conscious relation with Himself.[37] It is true that the very act of bringing something in relationship presupposes the existence of duality, but in the case of Parama Śiva, the sole Reality, the question of something existing apart from Him does not arise. Parama Śiva, therefore, never experiences complete duality between Himself as the Knower (*aham*) and His self-manifestation as the object (*idam*), as he always experiences them to be bound by a thread of unity. Thus the duality of His self-manifestation as the universe is always revealed in His experience (*parāmarśa*) as it were, in the background of an all-embracing Unity (*advaita*).

The *Kriyā śakti* is that aspect of divine Śakti exercising which the Supreme Lord manifests Himself as the uuniverse, assuming any and every role (*bhūmikā*), and thus directly causes the manifestation of His Divine Glory as the universe (*viśva*).[38]

---

[32] Tan. Sar, I, p. 6.

[33] T.S. I, p. 6.

[34] Cf. S.D. I, 19 Com. p. 17.

[35] S.D. II. 59 Com. p. 110.

[36] Sp. Kā I, p. 7 Com.

[37] S.D. I, 21, Comm. p. 18; T.S. I, p. 6.

[38] Cf. T.S. I, p. 6.

Being endowed with divine Freedom, the Supreme Lord has been described as *pañca kṛtyā kārī* (doer of five functions)[39] which the Supreme Lord is said to perform eternally. These are *nigraha*, (self limitation), *sṛṣṭi* (creation), *sthiti* (sustenance), *saṁhāra* (absorption) and *anugraha* (grace).[40] As these functions) go on in cyclic order, it is not possible to specify the starting point of functions. Looking from the point of view of creation however, *nigraha* may be considered as the starting point of His functions.

Nigraha consists in the imposition by the Supreme Lord of limitation on Himself (*ātma sañkoca*), as a result of which His absolute nature as the supreme Experiencing Principle (*Parāsaṁvid*) goes into the background, as it were, and He assumes monadic forms (*cidaṇu*).[41] This also results in the unfoldment of different *tattvas* or levels of creation constituting the entire cosmos. In the beginning, the universe thus unfolded appears only as the Supreme Lord's resolve (*saṅkalpa*) taking the form of His 'idea' only, but afterwards it assumes a gross form due to the operation of *Māyā śakti* and *Prakṛti śakti*.

Sthiti (sustenance) and *saṁhāra* (dissolution) are the two functions through which the universe manifested by Him is sustained in Himself, and then re-absorbed during the cosmic dissolution (*pralaya*).

Anugraha (grace), however, is an unique function that lies on a different plane. It consists in the Supreme Lord's dispensing grace to his self-limited spiritual forms, whereby He actually puts an end to His self-limited forms as it were.[42] It is the most important function through which the Supreme Lord restores the *cidaṇus* to their original divine status, that is *Śivatva*. The divine *anugraha* thus symbolises the doorway to the ultimate Destiny of all individuals which is, according to the Śaiva Tantras, *Śivatva* and not salvation (*mukti*).[43]

[39] Sp. Nir., III, 13 p. 66; STS V.I. Comm., p. 1.

[40] Pr. Hd., Su. 20 Comm.

[41] T.S. VIII, p. 77.

[42] *Ibid*, p. 79.

[43] Cf. MVT XII, 42.

It has been observed above that the Supreme Lord, during the period of creative activity, manifests Himself as the universe, which is nothing but the unfoldment of the different levels of creation or *tattvas*. The *Tantras* hold the total number of *tattvas* to be thirty-six, which have broadly been classified under two heads, technically called the *śuddha adhva* (pure way or realm) and the *aśuddha adhva* (impure way or realm).[44] The pure order (*śuddha adhva*) consists of five *tattvas* or levels of creation, viz *Śiva*, *Śakti*, *Sadāśiva*, *Īśvara* and *Śuddha Vidyā*, while the impure order (*asuddha adhva*) is constituted by thirty-one *tattvas*, beginning with the *māyā tattva* and extending up to the *pṛthvī tattva*.[45] In this connection, it would perhaps not be out of place to point out the distinguishing features of these two levels of creation which find mention in the Śāiva Tantras alone.

The *tattvas* constituting the pure realm are said to be manifested by the operation of divine Śakti in is pure form (*śuddha rūpa*), technically called *Mahāmāyā*.[46] The pure order, therefore, is said to exist in the realm of *Mahāmāyā*, and possesses all the characteristics of it. For instance, *Mahāmāyā* is the sphere in which the Supreme Lord experiences the universe epitomised by the term '*idam*' and manifested in pure ideal form. The universe then is subjective in character and spiritual (*cidrūpa*)[47] in content without any correspon-ding concrete objective representation.

The impure realm, on the other hand, is characterised by the operation of *Māyā śakti*, hence all the *tattvas* constituting this order bear the distinguishing characteristics of *Māyā*, viz limitedness and discreetness.[48] The operation of the *kriyā* aspect of the divine Śakti makes all the thirty-one *tattvas* assume concrete material form. The

---

[44] MVT II, 58; It may be pointed out here that at another place MVT classifies the entire creation under four heads — *pārthiva aṇḍa, prākṛta aṇḍa, māyīya aṇḍa* and *śākta aṇḍa*; see V. II, p. 49. See also *Paramārthasāra* V. 5.

[45] Cf. S.T.T.S. V. 4 Com.

[46] *Ibid.*

[47] *Ibid*, V. 3 Com., p. 3.

[48] STTS v. 5 Comm. p. 4.

universe then is no longer experienced by the Supreme Lord as something identical with Himself, as the operation of *Māyā śakti*, which is material by its very nature, hides the spiritual nature (*cidrūpa*) of the universe and also causes the rise of discreetness and multiplicity which are the distinguishing features of this realm.[49]

There is yet another level in the impure realm which is constituted by the *prakṛti tattva* and its twenty-three evolutes. This level is manifested due to the operation of *Prakṛti śakti*, hence it is held to be the grossest material form of creation.[50] Since the *Śaivāgamas* accept the scheme of creation as envisaged in the Sāṅkhya system and also the nature of the twenty-three *tattvas* with minor variations here and there, we refrain from giving a detailed description here.

We may however conclude by observing that all these thirty-six levels of creation which constitute the entire range of creation are contained in seminal form in the Supreme Lord, who is its Creator, Sustainer and Experiencer.

---

[49] *Parāpraveśikā* p. 7.

[50] STTS v.

~CHAPTER IV~

Nature of Man
in the Śaiva Śākta Tantras

Man occupies a pivotal position in all schools of Indian philosophy. This is more so in the field of the spiritual discipline or *sādhanakriyā* because various modes of *sādhanakriyā* are prescribed for man in bondage, different ways of spiritual ascent are laid down for him only. Man is the central figure in all schemes of creation and the Tantras are no exception to this.[1]

Man, a self-manifested form of the Supreme Reality

The conception of man differs from system to system. In the dualistic systems, he occupies a somewhat subordinate position to the Supreme Reality. In the monistic systems of thought, he is regarded to be one and identical with the Supreme Reality. The Śaiva Tantras which advocate a purely monistic philosophy are not in favour of a mere affirmation of the ontological non-difference between the individual and the Supreme Reality, but they take a step forward and declare that man is only a replica of the Supreme Reality, Parama Śiva, who actually assumes and manifests Himself as the multiplicity of individual beings and their objects of enjoyment.[2]

It has already been observed that Parama Śiva, in order to make multiplicity — the universe — to appear, imposes limitations on His infinite *svarūpa*, exercising His divine Freedom. As a result of this act of self-limitation (*ātmasaṁkoca or ātmanigraha*), His absolute

---

[1] Cf. Madhva philosophy of Vedānta.

[2] Par Sāra. v. 6 com. p. 18; Par. Carcā. v. 3.

Nature is obscured, His Divinity gets veiled, and He appears as a countless number of *pramātās* and *prameyas*, etc, on different levels of creation.[3] His *vyāpaka svarūpa* (pervasive nature) gets eclipsed, and He assumes the form of the spiritual monad (*cidaṇu*).[4] In this form, He is not able to experience His Divine Nature (*svarūpa*) characterised by such qualities as omnipotence (*sarvakartṛtva*), omniscience (*sarvajñatva*), self-contentment (*pūrṇatva*), eternity (*nityatva*) and freedom (*svatantrya*). This self-limitation (*ātma saṅkoca*), which follows directly from the operation of *nigraha* (one of the five *krityas* described before) is technically called the *āṇavamala*.[5] The manifestation of the *cidaṇus*, in fact, marks the beginning of the manifestation of individual beings in whom a distinct personality develops for the first time, and hereafter they acquire the fitness to being called individual beings. In this form, the individual being is incapable of experiencing his real divine nature, hence the *āṇavamala* is described as being of the nature of non-cognition (*akhyāti*).[6]

Defilements (*malas*), the cause for the manifestation of limited beings

Āṇavamala

In this connection it may be pointed out that, though the act of self-limitation is one and unique, the *āṇavamala* associated with every individual being is said to be manifold as in nature.[7] And it is held for this reason that when the *āṇavamala* is destroyed in one with the influx of the divine grace (*anugraha*) in him, it does not lead to the destruction of *āṇavamala* in all. The *āṇavamala* is the fundamental *mala* (*mūla mala*) which is responsible for the very existence of individual beings, and as such, it is said to be *āntara* or internal.[8]

---

3 Par. Carcā. v. 3, 6.

4 Tan. Al Ah. ix, v. 144-45.

5 *Mala* literally means defilement. The *āṇavamala* is the basic defilement in the form of self-contraction. Par. Sār v. 16, p. 45.

6 Cf. Tan. Āl. Ah. 1, v. 87-18 Com. p. 73 ff.

7 *Ibid.*, Āh. I x, v. 63 Com. p. 61 ff.

8 Par. Sār. v. 24 Com., p. 55.

The veiling of the individual being by *āṇavamala* is responsible for his experience of not-self (*anātmā*) in self (*ātmā*), which is technically called the *pauruṣa ajñāna*.[9] It is named the *pauruṣa ajñāna* (spiritual ignorance) because it has its locus in the *puruṣa* or self-contracted *cidaṇu* (spiritual monad) as different from the *bauddha ajñāna* (intellectual ignorance) which has locus in the intellect (*buddhi*) of the individual being.[10] A word of explanation is necessary to clarify this, which has no parallel in other well known orthodox systems.

It is said that the Supreme Lord, prior to his self-projection as the universe in exercise of his Divine Freedom, experiences Himself as the Pure subject (*śuddha aham*) in the absence of a second. This objectless self-experience (*pratyavamarśa*) as *Aham*[11] is said to be the highest self-experience of the Supreme Lord on the level of *Śiva tattva*, which is regarded as the apex in the hierarchy of *tattvas*. On the level of *Sadāśiva tattva*, however, this self-experience of the Supreme Lord takes the form of '*ahamidam*'[12] in which the pure object symbolised by the '*idam*', representing the entire cosmos in ideal form, emerges owing to the functioning of *icchā śakti*. Subsequently, on the level of the *Īśvara tattva*, the aspect of pure object (*idam*) in the Supreme Lord's self-experience gains prominence, and it assumes the form of '*idameva Aham*' (This is I).[13] In the succeeding step, i.e. the level of *śuddha vidyā*, both the aspects of pure Subject (*aham*) and pure Object (*idam*) in His self-experience become balanced as it were, and it assumes the form of *aham-idam* (I am this).[14] Here it may be pointed out that up to this level, the Divine Śakti in its pure form, technically called Mahāmāyā, functions to make the different levels of Pure Order (*śuddha adhva*)[15] manifest in the self-experience

9 Tan. Sār. I, . 3.

10 Tan, Sār. Ah. I, p.

11 Comparable to well-known Upaniṣadic saying '*So 'ham*'. Cf. Author's article on the 'Concept of Pūrṇāhamtā' in the *Corpus of Indian Studies*, Calcutta, 1980 pp. 153-64. See also I.P.V. III, 1, 3 com., p. 223 (Bhāskari Ed).

12 *Ibid.* 13 *Ibid.*, p. 224. 14 *Ibid.*

15 S.T.T.S., v. 2, p. 2.

of the Supreme Lord, hence He does not experience dichotomy between pure Subject and pure Object in his self-experience.

But with the functioning of *Māyā śakti*, which is only the materialised form of the Divine Śakti, the self-experience of the Supreme Lord undergoes a radical change. He no longer experiences Himself as pure Subject and His self-projected form as pure Object, both held in identity (*abheda sambandha*). The operation of *Māyā śakti*, which is responsible for the rise of discreteness and differentiation, brings about further limitation, and causes the disappearance of both the aspects of pure Subject (*aham*) and pure Object (*idam*) simultaneously in His self-experience. A vacuum is thus created, as it were, in His self-experience,[16] which is subsequently filled by the rise of the aspect of object (*idam*) or not-self on the level of *Māyā*, and its splitting into the limited subject and limited object. The Supreme Lord, on this level, becomes totally bereft of His divine Essence and powers, and is reduced to the form of a limited subject, technically called *paśu pramātā* (experiencer in bondage).[17]

The Supreme Lord in the form of *paśu pramātā* is not able to have his ego-experience (*ahaṁbodha*) in his pure Self as that has already disappeared owing to the imposition of self-limitation (*ātmasaṅkoca*)[18] and His simultaneously veiling by *Māyā*. Hence he has his ego-experience in the not-self, i.e. *idam*, represented by the body, etc. This is technically called the *pauruṣa ajñāna*.[19]

Since the *pauruṣa ajñāna* is consequent on the individual's self-contraction and covering by *āṇavamala*, it can be destroyed only after the termination of self-contraction and the consequent annihilation of *āṇavamala* in the individual being. It has been, therefore, held that the descent of Divine Grace alone is capable of nullifying the self-limitation, which arises from the imposition of limitation by the Supreme Lord. It may therefore be regarded as co-terminus with the manifestation and dissolution of individual beings in creation.

---

[16] Cf. I.P.V. III, 1, 6 Com. p. 229 (Bhāskarī Ed).

[17] *Ibid*., III, 1, 7 Com. p. 230 (Bhāsarī Ed).

[18] Cf. Ibid III, 1, 8 Com., p. 233-234.

[19] T.S. Ah. I, p. 1.

It has been observed that Parama Śiva is both omniscient and omnipotent, so that perfect knowledge (*pūrṇa jñāna*) and the freedom of act (*svātantrya*) constitute the two principal aspects of His absolute true nature (*svarūpa*). So long as He is not affected by the *aṇavamala*, these two essential aspects of His divine nature remain coalesced as it were,[20] in such a way that they are indistinguishable in His pure nature. But, as soon as He is covered by the self-imposed *āṇavamala*, these two aspects of His nature appear as differentiated and affected severely by limitation (*saṅkoca*), with the result that two distinct types of *cidaṇus* appear, with one of the aspects of their *svarūpa*, viz *jñāna* and *kriyā* affected by limitation.[21] The *cidaṇus* whose *kriyā* aspect of their nature is affected by the *āṇavamala*, which deprives them of their freedom of act (*svātantrya*) are technically called *vijñānākalas*.[22] The *vijñānākalas* are thus also a type of limited beings who retain consciousness of their real nature, but are bereft of their power of act or *svātantrya*, the essence of their divinity. Hence they are classed under *paśu pramātās*.[23]

There are other *cidaṇus* in whom the *āṇavamala* obscures the knowledge (*jñāna* or *bodha*) aspect of their pure nature, hence they are oblivious of it. The *kriyā* aspect of their nature, however, is not affected by the *āṇavamala*,[24] and it is this which induces them to undergo further involution. With the *kriyā* aspect remaining intact in them after their association with the *āṇavamala*, they cannot remain immobile in one state, the state of unembodied existence. They undergo further involution in *Māyā* to give, as it were, *Kriyā śakti* an opportunity of expression, and assume an appropriate kind of psycho-physical body apparatus (*deha yantra*).

The *āṇavamala* is thus of two kinds — one found in the disembodied beings, viz *vijñānakala*, and the other responsible for the manifestation of embodied beings, technically called *śakalas*,

---

[20] Cf. IPV III ii 4-5 comm., p. 248 (Bhāskarī Ed).

[21] Sat. Trim Tat. San.

[22] *Ibid.*, III, (ii) 7 comm., p. 249.

[23] *Ibid.*, III, (ii) 8 comm., p. 252.

[24] I.P.V. III, (ii) 4, p. 248 (Bhāskarī Ed.).

undergoing repeated transmigrations, both vertical as in involution in the higher-lower levels of existence, and horizontal from one gross physical body to another.

Māyīya mala

As the second type of *cidaṇus* undergo involution in the domain of *Māyā śakti*, which is described as the universal power of obscuration (*tirodhānakarī*),[25] she enwraps them with the result that their nature get further obscured. The veiling by *Māyā* is technically called the *māyīya mala*.[26]

Māyā is not alone in accomplishing the task of obscuration. It brings into operation five other forces of limitation, technically called *kañcukas*.[27] As these *kañcukas* (lit. integuments) enwrap the individual being, Śiva's divine powers as the Supreme Lord, which were indicative of His divine glory, are transformed into five principles of limitation (*kañcukas*) viz. *kalā*, *vidyā*, *rāga*, *kāla* and *niyati*. A word of explanation is necessary to understand the nature of five *kañcukas*.

As we have already observed above, the Supreme Lord, endowed with divine freedom, has omnipotence (*sarvakartṛtva*) as expression of His divine nature. This aspect of His divine power, when contracted by self-imposed limitation (*nigraha*) and obscured by *Māyā*, is reduced to the limited power of authorship in the *cidaṇu*, technically called *kalā*.[28] The Supreme Lord becomes 'drowsy' (*supta*)[29] as it were, as a result of this change. The omniscience (*sarvajñatva*) is another aspect of Supreme Lord's divine nature, which, undergoing limitation (*sañkoca*) and obscuration by *Māyā* is transformed into the limited power of knowledge in the individual being, technically called *vidyā*.[30] This results in the reduction of the Supreme Lord's

25 I.P.V., III, (i) 7, p. 231.

26 *Ibid.*, III, (ii) 9, p. 253.

27 *Ibid.*, III, (i) 9 com., p. 235-38.

28 S.T.T.S., v. 8, p.

29 T.S., Ah. VIII, p.

30 Sat. Trim Tat. San., v. 9.

infinite power of knowledge into the limited power of knowledge, whereby the limited experiencer gets only a vague, undefined and discrete view of the objects of knowledge.

Being endowed with divine freedom, the Supreme Lord, who is full-in-Himself (*paripūrṇa*), feels Himself ever self-satisfied and self-contented (*tṛpta*) so that the does not feel the necessity of moving out. This aspect of His divine nature, when contracted by self-limitation (*nigraha*) and obscured by *Māyā śakti*, is transformed into the limited power of interest in a *cidaṇu*, technically called *rāga*.[31]

The Supreme Lord, as transcendent Absolute (*viśvottīrṇa*), is immutable and beyond time, space and causality. This aspect of His divine nature, when affected by self-imposed limitation (*saṅkoca*) and *Māyā*, undergoes a radical transformation in the *cidaṇu*, as a result of which he becomes subject to limitation in time; this is called technically *kāla*.[32]

The Supreme Lord in His immanent aspect is all-pervasive (*vyāsaka*). This aspect of His divine nature is reduced in the *cidaṇu* to the limited power of confinement in space by the self-imposed contraction and *Māyā*. This is technically called *niyati*,[33] which is also held responsible for subjecting him to the cause-effect relationship.

Thus these five *kañcukas*, which serve as the powers of concealment, are transformations of the Supreme Lord's divine powers, due to a self-imposed contraction (*sra-saṅkoca*) and the operation of *Māyā śakti*. They represent five snares (*pāśa*) by which the Supreme Lord is bound and reduced to the limited *cidaṇu*. Here it must be pointed out that, although the five *kañcukas* are regarded by the Śaiva texts as 'progeny' of *Māyā tattva*,[34] yet they are said to have independent existence, and therefore they are enumerated separately in the list of thirty-six *tattvas* admitted by this school.

---

31 Sat. Trim Tat. San., v. 10.

32 *Ibid.*, v. 11.

33 *Ibid.*, v. 12.

34 *Kashmir Shaivism*, p. 75.

Thus, we find that the obscuration of individual beings by the *Māyā tattva* does not remain confined to the mere hiding of their divine essence; it also brings about drastic changes in their nature (*svarūpa*), which follow obscuration as a natural corollary.[35] For instance, the veiling of a *cidaṇu* by *māyīyamala* results in his ensnaring by different kinds of *pāśa* when he experiences differentiation and discreetness (*bahutva*) all over instead of oneness and unity. This experience of differentiation by the *cidaṇus* however remains indistinct and hazy in that stage,[36] because the *cidaṇus* are then devoid of ego-sense (*ahaṁbodha*) following the imposition of *āṇavamala*. But, as they get back, as it were, their ego sense on their being associated with a physical body, they begin experiencing discreteness and differentiation between subject and object, which characterises all worldly experience.

The *māyīya mala*, like the *āṇavamala*, is beginningless, though destructible. Its destruction can be brought about by an individual *cidaṇu* through his persistent intense endeavour.

Kārma mala

As the task of concealment of the individual beings' divine nature is accomplished by *māyīya mala*, the *kārmic* seeds[37] lying dormant in *Māyā* get attached to the *cidaṇus* (individual beings). The *karmabījas* are products of subtle residual impressions of the past *karmas* performed by all the *cidaṇus* in embodied form, which lie embedded in *Māyā*. As the *cidaṇus* enter into the realm of *Māyā*, *kārmic* seeds cling to the individual *cidaṇu*, and they awaken in him a desire for performance of *karma* (*karmavāsanā*), which, in turn, impels him to associate himself with an appropriate kind of psycho-physical organism, i.e. a body-apparatus (*dehayantra*) produced out of *Prakṛti* and its constituent *tattvas*. As the association of an indi-

35 I.P.V. III, ii, 8, p. 252-53 (Bhāskarī Ed.).

36 *Ibid*.

37 Tan. Al. Ah. IX, 88, Comm., p. 75.

vidual *cidaṇu* with a body-apparatus results in further obscuration of his true nature, the *karmabījas* are regarded as being of the nature of a veil, and are technically called the *kārmamala*.[38]

The *kārmamala* is thus the root cause of an individual being's conjunction with a body-apparatus.[39] It is a relatively permanent *mala*, as it is not destroyed with the falling off of one body-apparatus. It is said to persist through the births and deaths of an individual. It is beginningless (*anādi*), though destructible through intense personal efforts of the individual.

Associated with every embodied individual, *kārmamala* is said to be manifold in nature, so much so that it is unique in every individual being. It is this characteristic feature of *kārmamala* which bestows on the individual being a distinct personality,[40] notwithstanding the fact that all *sakalas* (embodied beings) are bound by the same three *malas*, viz, *āṇava*, *mayīya* and *kārmamala*.

Besides this, the *kārmamala* is also said to determine the type of body with which an individual *cidaṇu* is to be associated.[41] The Śaiva texts mention three different kinds of body-apparatus, viz *daiva śarira* (super-human), *mānuṣa śarīra* (human) and *tiryag-śarīra* (sub-human). Of these, the body-apparatus of the superhuman and subhuman beings are called *bhogāyatanas* or *bhoga deha* (lit. vehicle for enjoyment or experience) as they serve the purpose of enjoyment only, while the body-apparatus of human beings is known as *karma deha* as they are suitable for the performance of actions (*karma*).

Insofar as the constitution of these two types of body-apparatuses are concerned, it appears that there is not any substantial difference in their constitution, excepting that in the case of individual beings possessing *bhoga deha*, their ego-sense is latent, while in the individual beings having *karma-deha* it is manifest and guides their activity. Hence performance of *karma* by them causes the vertical

---

38 I.P.V. III, ii, 5 Com., P. 249 (Bhāskarī Ed).

39 *Ibid*, III, ii, 10 Com., p. 254-55.

40 *Ibid*.

41 I.P.V. III, ii, 10, p. 253 (Bhāskarī Ed).

movement in the different hierarchy of levels, while in the former, possessing *bhogadeha*, there is no scope for such movement.

The individual beings' association with a body due to *kārma-mala* causes the rise of *bauddha ajñāna* (intellectual ignorance), which is in the form of the false identification of not-self with self (*anātmani ātmabodha*) as has been described above. It is said to be conceptual by nature (*vaikalpika*) as it lies in the *buddhi* of the individual.[42] It is temporary as it arises with the individual being's association with a body-apparatus, and is terminated with his dissociation with the body.

The Śaiva texts admit two kinds of bodies, the subtle and the gross. As in other orthodox systems of Indian philosophy, the subtle body, is technically called *ātivāhika deha* (lit. body for carrying the individual being from one gross body to another).[43] The Advaita Śaiva texts use another term to signify the subtle body, viz *puryaṣṭaka* (body made of eight component elements). The subtle body is relatively permanent as the individual being is associated with it in the beginning of creation. The Tāntrika texts generally subscribe to the view held by orthodox systems like Sāṁkhya-yoga, Vedānta, etc, that the subtle body is the locus of different kinds of residual impressions of *karma* (*karma saṁskāras*) performed by the individual in embodied condition, and it is these *karma saṁskāras* which cause transmigration as well as the vertical movement on the different levels of creation.

The gross physical body, constituted by the five *mahābhūtas* (gross physical elements), is a temporary body, which the individual takes in accordance with the residual impressions of actions (*karma saṁskāras*). The gross physical body can be roughly of four kinds, according to whether it arises from embryo (*jarāyuja*), egg (*aṇḍaja*), sweat (*svedaja*) or earth by sprouting (*udbhija*).

---

[42] T.S.I.

[43] Jan. Mar. Vicāra, p. 2.

~CHAPTER V~

Spiritual Discipline (Sādhana Kriyā) and the Supreme Goal

It has been shown in the foregoing pages that the Supreme Lord, Parama Śiva, exercising His Divine Freedom on the different levels of creation, manifests Himself as *paśupramātā* (fettered beings). We have also seen how He, as a fettered being, is covered by three kinds of defilements (*mala*) which make him forget his divine essence, and force him to undergo repeated transmigrations in this world and experience the fruits of his deeds.

We have also observed that the self-manifestation by the Supreme Lord as fettered beings represents His descent or involution (*avaroha*) on the material plane, seeing things from His point of view. Now the question arises, how can he evolve from his present position as fettered being to ascend (*āroha*) gradually to the highest level of perfection to achieve the Supreme Goal.

Sri Aurobindo, in his *magnum opus* 'Life Divine' has given the answer. He observes that evolution is a natural universal process, which is going on eternally and imperceptibly in the insentient and sentient world ever since the involution of pure spirit into matter. This process is a logical corollary to the process of involution when the world was first manifested.

Evolution (*aroha*) — involuntary and as a result of spiritual discipline

The Śaiva and Śākta Tantras are ardent advocates of the theory of evolution not only in the field of creation but also in the spiritual world. They are probably the first to propound the theory that a process of involuntary evolution of embodied beings is going on eternally in creation — lower animals evolving and ascending to higher levels of creation, man evolving and gradually rising up in the hierarchy of 'higher' beings, ending up in the achievement of the Supreme Goal. Of course, this theory presupposes the existence of a hierarchical order in creation, to which both the Śaiva and Śākta Tantras subscribe.

The Śaivācāryas of Kāśmīra, who have given their own interpretation of the Śaiva Tantra, take a step further in ascribing a positive role to the divine Freedom of the Supreme Lord. Though they generally do not oppose the theory of natural evolution operating eternally in creation, still, being ardent advocates of divine Freedom, they do not attach much importance to the evolutionary process. According to them, the process of natural evolution of the embodied human individual to the supreme spiritual end is of little value to one who aspires to reach the Supreme Goal in his lifetime. He cannot afford to wait indefinitely and suffer in his present embodied condition, for natural evolutionary process is painfully slow and a time-consuming process. Hence the *śaivācāryas* seek refuge in the divine Freedom of the Supreme Lord, which operates without any restriction or precondition, and can hasten the ascent of the individual aspirant. It is for this reason that the spiritual aspirant, being in a fettered condition (*pāśabaddha paśu*), is advised to attune himself to the divine will of the Supreme Lord which is omnipresent in creation and operates imperceptibly, and seek its help to disentangle himself from the worldly web. This line of approach in spiritual discipline was first advocated by the followers of the Spanda School of Śaiva thought who, in turn, were probably influenced by the Kaulas belonging to the Śākta stream of thought.

All spiritual aspirants, however, are not capable of obtaining help from the divine Will directly, as it functions independently of individual aspirations and needs. Hence, it is laid down that the spiritual aspirants should follow certain yogic disciplines and perform certain yogic exercises suited to their individual needs and in consonance with their temperaments, in order to embark on the spiritual journey.

Steps leading to the attainment of the Supreme Goal

The Tantric texts therefore formulate as many as ten steps, which ordinarily lead an individual aspirants to his spiritual goal. These are (i) purgation of all kinds of defilements (*malanivṛtti*), (ii) infusion of divine Grace and initiation of the individual (*śaktipāta* and *dīkṣā*), (iii) destruction of spiritual ignorance (*pauruṣa ajñāna*), (iv) attainment of the capacity for obtaining spiritual wisdom through the hearing of *Āgama vākya* (words of Āgamic texts) from the spiritual teacher (*guru*), (v) the rise of intellectual knowledge (*bauddha jñāna*), (vi) simultaneous destruction of intellectual ignorance (*bauddha ajñāna*), (vii) attainment of liberation in embodied condition (*jīvanmukti*), (viii) destruction of ripened fruits of past actions (*prārabdha karma*) through enjoyment (*bhoga*), (ix) the rise of spiritual knowledge (*pauruṣa jñāna*) simultaneously with the falling off of the psycho-physical body (*deha*), and (x) achievement of the Supreme Goal, *Śivatva*.

We propose to consider these steps of spiritual ascent one by one in the following paragraphs. Let us first take up for examination the first step, namely purgation. In the foregoing pages we have discussed in detail the nature of three kinds of defilement which envelop every embodied individual existing on the different levels of *Māyā*, i.e. different *tattvas* of the impure realm (*aśuddha adhva*). We have also indicated that with the exception of the *āṇavamala*, the fundamental *mala* arising out of self-imposed limitation, all other kinds of *malas* (defilements) can be eradicated by an individual through his personal efforts in the form of discipline (*sādhanā*). Or else, all these defilements become mature in course of time, leading to their eventual destruction. But this process of maturation in which *Kāla śakti* (time-force) and other unseen factors play a great role is time-consuming. It can, however, be accelerated by an individual being through his personal efforts. In the normal state of bondage, when the individual being is covered by three kinds of defilement, his intellect (*citta*) remains coated with different layers of impurities, technically called *kaṣāyas* or *kleṣas* (lit. colours and residual impressions of *karmas* and *vāsanās*). The cleaning or purgation of the psycho-physical frame, i.e. the body including the intellect, is essential for the spiritual aspirant in order to have a true glimpse of his real Self. The purgation is, therefore, the first step in the journey of a human individual to the supreme goal, and as such, has universally been acknowledged to be so. For this, the orthodox systems of Indian philosophy such as Sāṁkhya-Yoga, Advaita Vedānta, etc prescribe an eight-limbed (*aṣṭānga*) ethico-psychological discipline (*yoga*), such as, five kinds of abstentions (*yama*), control of the senses (*niyama*), posture (*āsana*), regulation of inhalation and exhalation of breath (*prāṇāyāma*), withdrawal in gradual steps of the sense-organs from the worldly objects (*pratyāhāra*), fixation of attention on one object (*dhāranā*), meditation (*dhyāna*) and concentration (*samādhi*).[1] These limbs of yogic exercise propounded first by the Sāṁkhya and Yoga systems are universally accepted as means for cleansing the intellect, the chief instrument of self-knowledge and self-realisation. Since a tainted intellect cannot reflect a clear 'picture' of the real Self, purgation is considered as a necessary first step towards spiritual self-realisation by almost all systems of Indian philosophical thought.

But the *śaivācāryas* of Kashmir, who are ardent advocates of the doctrine of divine Freedom, do not consider the practice of this eight-limbed yogic exercise to be essential for purgation. According to them, purgation is achieved by the aspirant through the descent of divine grace in appropriate measure. As such it is not dependent on individual efforts. Hence they lay stress or the descent of divine grace, technically called *śaktipāta*, which plays a crucial role in

[1] Cf. *Yogasūtra* of Patañjali II, 29. It may be pointed out here that the *Yoga Sūtras* prescribe *abhyāsa* (repeated practice) and *vairāgya* (total non-attachment) as the chief modes of yogic discipline, but these are meant for the highest class of spiritual aspirants, while the above are prescribed for ordinary aspirants.

spiritual discipline. Though purgation takes place with the infusion of divine Grace in the individual, the *śaivācaryas* in their eagerness to give supreme place to divine Freedom consider the descent of divine Grace to be the starting point in spiritual journey of the individual aspirant. We propose to take up the concept of *guru* (spiritual teacher) and *dīkṣā* (initiation) later in two separate chapters.

Here, it may be pointed out for the sake of clarification that purgation in an individual aspirant takes place in two phases, one prior to the descent of divine Grace on the individual being, and the other after its descent. So far as the purgation prior to the infusion of ivine Grace in the individual is concerned, it can be achieved through the practice of the eight-limbed yogic exercises by an individual, or it can take place consequent to the destruction of *māyīya* and *kārma* defilements in course of time. In both these cases, purgation prepares an individual for receiving the divine Grace in an appropriate measure, which is indicated by its intensity. It is thus a preparatory step, though not an essential step in the eyes of the *śaivācāryas* of Kashmir advocating divine Freedom.

Purgation effected by the descent of divine Grace may be instantaneous, as is in the case of the highest class of aspirants, who are not required to make any efforts to achieve the supreme Goal, or alternatively, it may be in gradual steps as is the case with the lesser perfect classes of human aspirants. The purgation is linked with the destruction of *māyīya* and *kārma malas*, which may be instantaneous or gradual. We shall revert to this under the heading 'Śaktipāta' in chapter VII.

The succeeding step after the infusion of divine Grace through the medium of *Guru* and initiation by him (which shall be dealt with separately in the next chapter) leads to the destruction of *pauruṣa ajñāna* (spiritual ignorance). This needs some explanation as the Śaiva texts of Kashmir admit two distinct kinds of ignorance: spiritual ignorance (*pauruṣa ajñāna*), and *bauddha ajñāna* or intellectual ignorance.

The *pauruṣa ajñāna* is the foundational ignorance which arises out of the self-imposed limitation or self contraction (*ātmasaṅkoca*) by the Supreme Lord at the beginning of the creative cycle (*sṛṣṭi*). As a result of this, he is enwrapped by *āṇava mala*, which is nothing but self-contraction, and he experiences himself as bereft of all his divine powers (*aiśvarya*) when he assumes the form of spiritual monad (*cidaṇu*). This also makes him experience himself as an 'I' (*aham*) in a not-'I' (*idam*), the real divine Essence having been eclipsed as a sequel to self-contraction. Thus the *pauruṣa ajñāna* or spiritual ignorance is an offshoot of the self-imposed limitation or his envelopment by the *aṇava mala*.

This being the case, spiritual ignorance cannot have intellect as its seat, as intellect (*citta* or *buddhi*) comes into being much later. This ignorance is, therefore, considered to be non-intellectual, or spiritual by nature. It therefore follows that its destruction cannot depend on individual efforts, which can operate up to the level of the intellect only. It is, therefore, held that spiritual ignorance is destroyed by the descent of divine Grace, which destroys also the *āṇava mala* simultaneously.

After the individual aspirant obtains freedom from both the *āṇava mala* and spiritual ignorance, he develops in him the capacity for gaining spiritual knowledge, technically called *śuddha vidyā* (pure spiritual knowledge), or *sattarka* from the words of the spiritual teacher (*sadguru*), or from his study of scriptural texts (*sadāgama*). In rare cases, this knowledge may arise automatically from within in such aspirants who are completely free from all kinds of defilements like *āṇava*, *mayīya*, etc. Such aspirants belong to the higher class of *sādhakas*, and are called *sāmsiddhika sādhakas* (inborn perfect beings). The description of the function of Īśvara as given in the *Vyāsa bhāṣya* on the *Yoga sūtra*, namely, that the sole function of God is to shower grace on the afflicted persons (*bhūtānugraha*),[2] fully applies to this perfect class of *sādhakas*. This step is, therefore, called as the

[2] *Yoga Sūtra* 1. The *Tripurārahasya* says about such perfect beings: *uttamānaṁ tu vijñānaṁ guru-śāstrānapekṣam.*

development of the capacity for *sadāgama śravaṇa* (hearing words of spiritual wisdom). Since the intellect of the spiritual aspirant in this stage is absolutely pure on account of the infusion of divine Grace and the consequent destruction of the *āṇavamala* as well as the eradication of spiritual ignorance, therefore the moment the aspirant hears words of spiritual wisdom from the mouth of his *guru* or gains knowledge from his study of the *sadāgamas*, his pure intellect is at once illumined by the light of the pure knowledge of his real Essence. This knowledge, having its locus in the intellect, is obviously intellectual knowledge, and is therefore called *bauddha jñāna* or intellectual knowledge. It is, therefore, conceptual in nature and purely intuitive in character, owing to its rise in the purified intellect.

The rise of intellectual knowledge in the pure intellect of the spiritual aspirant signalises the end of the intellectual ignorance (*bauddha ajñāna*) which had till then covered the intellect. This is because intellectual knowledge and intellectual ignorance are mutually opposed to one another, and as such cannot co-exist. The annihilation of intellectual ignorance (*bauddha ajñāna*) by intellectual knowledge (*bauddha jñāna*) enables the spiritual aspirant to attain a state of perfection when he is free from two kinds of defilements, viz *āṇava* and *māyīya*, and is firmly established in his real divine nature. It is said that *prātibha jñāna* (pure intuitive knowledge) arises from within the purified intellect of the aspirant. As this knowledge is not derived from any external source, it has been described as *anaupadeśika mahājñāna* (great knowledge nor derived from any verbal instruction [*upadeśa*] by any external teacher, etc).

Such aspirants are said to achieve complete emancipation while still in an embodied condition, which is technically called *jīvanmukti*. The psycho-physical body in this state continues to exist on account of the continuance of seeds of *karma* which are ripe and start fruition, technically called *prārabdha karma saṁskāra*. This also means that *kārma mala* continues to exist in this state despite the destruction of *āṇava* and *māyīyamalas*, and hence the physical body continues to exist.

All schools of Indian philosophy including the Tāntrika believe that the *prārabdha karma* cannot be destroyed by any other means except through experiencing (*bhoga*) the fruits of actions. The Śaiva and Śākta schools with their emphasis on the divine grace make one exception. They hold that in extreme rare cases, where the divine grace descends in an extremely intense form, destruction of all the three kinds of defilements, viz the *āṇava*, *māyiya* and *kārma* — which includes *prārabdha karma* — is instantenous. Abhinavagupta in his *Tantrasāra* has cited the case of those rare *yogins* who, on being infused with divine Grace in extremely intense form, attain the supreme Goal — *Śivatva* — in a moment as it were, without having to practise any discipline whatsoever. Such privileged aspirants loose their physical body immediately after the infusion of divine Grace, and as such are only exceptions.

In most cases the union of the spiritual aspirants with the divine Essence takes place simultaneously with the influx of divine Grace in them, but the eradication of all kinds of ignorance takes place in gradual steps. Hence the supreme End is not reached by them at the same moment. In the intervening period between the infusion of divine Grace and the destruction of the physical body, they are firmly established in their divine Essence, and enjoy the fruits of liberation while existing in an embodied condition. This state of their existence is similar to that which may be called *jīvanmukti* (attainment of liberation in embodied state).

In his *Mahārtha Mañjarī*,[3] Maheśvarānanda describes *jīvanmukti* as a state in which there is perfect equilibrium between liberation and enjoyment. Śrīratnadeva says that the states of enjoyment and liberation are not identical in essence, and as such are not seen together under normal conditions; but when in special cases these are found together perfectly balanced, this state is called *jīvanmukti*.[4] The spiritual aspirant in that state participates in all the normal activities

---

[3] *Op. cit.*, p. 137.

[4] Cf. *Bhuktir-vāpyatha muktiśca nānyatraikapadārthataḥ* |
bhuktimukti ubhe dver viśeṣe prakīrtite ||

in life, but, at the same time, experiences the world around him to be his self-expansion, an expression of his Divine Glory.[5]

The Sahajīyā Buddhists, it may be mentioned here, believed too in the existence of this state, as is evident from their statement that the spiritual aspirant experiences *mahāsukha* (great Bliss) when he is able to control the movement of the sun (*sūrya*) and the moon (*candra*) in the *nāḍīs* (channels) existing in his body, and also succeeds in enkindling the light of *bodhicit* (consciousness). They further point out that the attainment of this condition leads to his achievement of both *bhava* (worldly life) and *nirvāṇa* all at once.

The attainment of *jīvanmukti* does not mean the achievement of the journey's End, for so long as the aspirant continues to exist in an embodied condition, he is enveloped by the *kārma mala* which in fact is the same as *prārabdha karma*. As a consequence of this, the *pauruṣa jñāna* (spiritual knowledge) cannot arise in him. The continuance of the physical body is an obstacle in the way of the rise of *pāūruṣa jñāna*, which is not conceptual by its very nature. Hence it is said that the association of the aspirant with his physical body must cease before he can have the perfect integral self-experience of his divine Essence, which is the same as the *pauruṣa jñāna*. The *pauruṣa jñāna* is said to be in the form of self-experience as *pūrṇāhamtā*. This is the Supreme Goal, the ultimate End.

[5] Cf. *Sarvo mamāyaṁ baibhavaḥ*.

~Chapter VI~

Śāktipāta and Guru

Śāktipāta and its role in spiritual discipline

As has been observed in the foregoing pages, all Tantric Śaiva schools of thought agree in postulating the Supreme Reality, the Parama Śiva as performing eternally five functions, technically called *kṛtyas*, viz., *tirodhāna* (self-limitation), *sṛṣṭi* (creation), *sthiti* (maintenance), *saṁhāra* or *pralaya* (dissolution) and *anugraha* (grace).[1] These functions, which the Supreme Lord is said to perform in cyclic order, are very important from the point of view of the manifestation of the world as well as from the point of view of *sādhanakriyā* (spiritual discipline), for it is the generally accepted view of all shades of Tantric tradition whether *Śaiva*, *Śākta* or *Vaiṣṇava* that the Supreme Lord, out of His Free Will, assumes different roles of subjects, objects (*grāhaka*, *grāhya*) and means of their enjoyment (*bhoga-sādhana*) in creation.[2] The created world, thus, represents a sort of involution of the Supreme Spirit, i.e. the Supreme Lord, in the realms of matter, a descent.[3] The Tāntrika systems also subscribe to the theory of evolution as a natural phenomenon, which is continuously going on in creation. This concept, which is totally absent in all other orthodox systems of Indian philosophy such as Sāṁkhya-Yoga, Vedānta, etc, appears to be based only on scientific principles, but is also a natural corollary to the functioning of the ever-vibrating (*spandanaśīla*) Śakti responsible for the manifestation of Reality in ever-new forms.

---

[1] Pr. Hd., Sū 10, com.

[2] *Ibid.*, Sū 3, com. [3] *Ibid.*

The evolution of the individual being, which is said to be always going on ever since he was first manifested in creation, represents his ascent to the higher levels of creation. Its pace can however be accelerated by him by performing spiritual discipline or *sādhanā*,[4] culminating ultimately in the restoration of his essential divinity through divine union (*śāmbhava samāveśa*).

As the descent of the Supreme Lord in the realms of matter, i.e. creation, is purely volitional, arising as it does from the imposition of self-limitation, the ascent, which is a corresponding function of the Supreme Lord, must necessarily be a purely volitional act, depending on His Free Will to put an end to his self-imposed limitation (*ātmānugraha*). The Tantric texts, therefore, consider *tīrodhāna* to be the starting point in the creative cycle of the Supreme Lord's self-manifestation as Universe, and *anugraha* (grace) to be the closing point in that cycle. *Anugraha* or *śaktipāta* thus represents that function of the Supreme Lord whereby He restores himself from a monadic form (*cidaṇu*)[5] to His original Divine Nature (*svarūpa*), by nullifying the effects of *nigraha* (self-contraction) out of His own Free Will (*svatantra icchā*).[6] It is an eternal function of the Supreme Lord, signalising as it does the closing point in the cycle of creative process (*sṛṣṭikrama*), which itself is nothing but a mode of the Supreme Lord's self-manifestation,[7] His divine sport (*līlā*) looking from His point of view.

In the field of Tantra yoga, *anugraha* or *śaktipāta* plays a crucial role inasmuch as it marks the beginning of man's journey to the ultimate Goal which, according to the Śaiva Tantra, is not liberation (*mukti*), but restoration of His real divine nature, i.e. *Śivatva*.[8] Liberation or emancipation, in the Tantric view, is a negative concept which aims merely at the destruction of one's bonds, whereas the

4 I.P.V. III, ii. (Bhāskarī Ed.).

5 T.S. XI, p. 118.

6 Pr. Hd. sū 11 com.

7 T.S. XI, p. 118.

8 *Ibid.*

achievement of *Śivatva* is a positive concept[9] inasmuch as it results in not only the annihilation of various bonds (*pāśas*) which are responsible for his manifestation as a *paśu* (a fettered being) but also brings the manifestation of various divine powers in him that are the essence of His divine nature (*pārameśvarya*).

The Tantras believe that evolution, as a natural process, cannot take the fettered individual beyond the realm of matter, because it is essentially a material phenomenon. Even the individual being cannot cross the sphere of *prakṛti*, which is the grossest form of divine Śakti, through his intense personal efforts.[10] Hence *śaktipāta* (influx of divine Grace) is considered as indispensable for his upliftment into the realm of Spirit, i.e. *Mahāmāyā* or divine *Śakti* in pure spiritual form. It alone is capable of enabling the fettered being to cross the levels of *prakṛti* and enter into the realm of pure order that lays beyond *Māyā*.

There is yet another reason for regarding *śāktipāta* to be the starting point in man's ascent in the realm of pure Spirit. We have already observed that the individual being in bondage is enveloped by three kinds of *malas* (defilement), viz *āṇava*, *māyīya* and *kārma*.[11] The *āṇavamala* is the fundamental *mala* enveloping him, as it arises out of the imposition of self-limitation by the Supreme Lord. The *māyīyamala*, which is due to his being covered by *Māyā* and her five *kañcukas* (lit. sheaths),[12] deprives him of his essential divinity since it eclipses His divine powers such as omniscience, omnipotence etc.

---

[9] In this connection it may be mentioned here that the *Upaniṣads* use the term '*amṛtattva*' (lit. immortality) frequently to denote the highest goal of life in place of *mukti* (emancipation), which has seldom been used. In the eyes of the upaniṣadic seers, *mukti* appeared to be a smaller ideal while the achievement of *amṛtattva* was the supreme ideal, which also included enjoyment of the fruit of Self-knowledge *(ātmajñāna)*. Note also a similar distinction in the ideal of *ārhathood* and *bodhisattva* propagated by the Hīnayāna Buddhists and Mahāyāna Buddhists respectively.

[10] I.P.V., III, ii.

[11] See the author's article entitled "Pañca Kañcukas and Pañcakośas" in *Charudeva Shastri Felicitation Volume*, Delhi 1974, pp. 385-94.

[12] Pr. Hd. Su 9, com.

The *kārma mala,* which is due to his envelopment by *karmabījas* (*karma* in seed form) lying on the level of *Māyā* makes him assume an appropriate kind of psycho-physical body to satiate his desire for enjoyment. Of these three kinds of *malas,* which envelop all embodied individuals, the *āṇavamala* is the chief one, which can be annihilated only by the descent of divine grace (*śaktipāta*) on the individual being since this one is the product of the act of self-limitation (*ātmanigraha*) by the supreme Lord. Unless the *āṇavamala* is destroyed first,[13] and the self-imposed limitation is put an end to, the individual being cannot secure his entry to the realm of Spirit, i.e. *śuddha adhva*.

Being an eternal function of the Supreme Lord, the *anugraha* or *śaktipāta* flows eternally from the highest source, i.e. the Supreme Lord, but it is available only to a select few who have developed in course of time the capacity to receive it within them. Looking from the qualitative point of view, the divine grace received by the individual in bondage is always the same, but it differs quantitatively from one aspirant to another in proportion to their capacity[14] which, again, is directly dependent on the degree of perfection achieved by the individual through his personal efforts.

Abhinavagupta in his *Tantrāloka* speaks of nine kinds of divine grace based on its intensity.[15] He first classified grace under three broad heads, namely, most intense (*tīvra*), intense (*madhya*) and mild (*manda*), which are again classifed under these heads each — most intense, intense and mild — thus making nine kinds of divine grace received by as many kinds of recipient *sādhakas*. This can be explained on the analogy of rainwater falling from the clouds. The divine grace is like rainwater falling eternally from the highest source. Just as the amount of rainwater collected in different containers such as holes, pits, tanks, etc, depends on the size or capacity of the containers, in the same way the varying capacity of the individual

[13] T.S. XI, p. 119; also see M.V.T. I, 42-46, p. 5-6.

[14] T.S. XI, p. 114.

[15] *Ibid.*

recipient determines the intensity of grace received by an individual. If the intensity of grace were to exceed the capacity of the recipients, the result obviously would be bound to be disastrous for the *sādhaka*.

It can therefore be said that the intensity of divine grace received by an individual aspirant is the index of his progress in the spiritual path on one hand, and on the other, it also determines the amount of effort he would have to put in to achieve the supreme goal. There is intimate relationship between divine grace and individual endeavour, for the general rule is that the more intense the grace in an individual, the fewer endeavours it would entail on the part of the *sādhaka*. In other words, the *sādhaka* has to make good any deficiency in the intensity of divine grace received by him by his personal efforts in the same proportion as this deficiency, for the cumulative resultant of grace and effort has to be constant. The personal effort in this case means arduous paths of yogic *sādhanā*, which have been prescribed for different types of *sādhakas* based on the intensity of divine grace.

The Tantric texts mention some characteristic signs, which indicate the quantitative difference in the intensity of divine grace received by the individual aspirants. For instance, it s said that the aspirants who happen to receive divine grace in its most intense form (*tīvra tīvra śaktipāta*) immediately lose their body due to the destruction of ripened *karma* seeds (*prārabdha karma*) simultaneously. Just as the body of the individual is burnt in a moment on being struck by thunderbolt, in the same way the body of the recipient of divine grace in intense form is destroyed simultaneously with the infusion of grace, and he is said to achieve the Supreme Goal, viz *Śivatva*, without taking the trouble of performing any discipline.

But all aspirants are not fortunate enough to receive divine grace in most intense form. The aspirants who receive the divine grace in relatively less intense form than the former (i.e. *madhya tīvra śaktipāta*) continue to exist in an embodied form owing to the continuance of *prārabdha karma*, viz *sañcita* (accumulated *kārmic* seeds), while *sañcīyamāna karma* (*kārmic* seeds being accumulated) are immediately destroyed. As a consequence, the ignorance is not completely eradicated, but only the 'sheath' (*āvaraṇa*) aspect of ignorance is destroyed, the *vikṣepa* aspect remaining intact. This leads to the development of certain signs in the aspirants which indicate the influx of grace in them. For instance, the aspirant develops within him a unique kind of devotion (*bhakti*) towards the Supreme Being or God who draws him as it were near himself. Such aspirants in some cases obtain *mantra siddhi* (control over the potency of magical incantations). This helps in restoring their faith in the scriptural truths. They sometimes also develop the capacity of getting complete knowledge about any object which they perceive. In some cases, they are able to know the real import of the words of the *Śāstras*, which generally remain hidden to ordinary beings.

The infusion of divine grace in a relatively mild form (*manda tivra*) results in the development of an intense desire in the aspirants to go to a *sadguru* (real *guru*) for instruction and guidance in the spiritual path. We shall take up the nature and function of *guru* for examination in the following pages. It would suffice here to make a general observation regarding *guru*.

Broadly speaking, there are two types of *guru*. One, having established himself firmly in the divine Essence, is capable of leading others to the supreme Goal. Such *gurus*, as a rule, act in accordance with the divine will and are therefore called *sadguru*. But there are others who could not reach the supreme Goal but advanced considerably towards it and are conversant with the path of spiritual discipline and its pitfalls. Such *gurus*, though very helpful, are called *asad gurus*, i.e. *gurus* incapable of leading to the supreme Goal. We shall revert to this in the next section.

Here, it may be mentioned that the Tantric texts venerated by the Śaiva Siddhāntins consider that maturation of *malas* (*mala paripāka*) in an individual is the main factor for determining the descent of divine grace,[16] while the Tantric texts venerated by the Advaita Śaivites of Kashmir, laying their emphasis on the divine

[16] T.S. XI.

Freedom (*svātantrya*), do not postulate any condition for the influx of divine grace.[17] The *Mālinīvijayottara Tantra* clearly points out that to conceive of any condition responsible for the descent of divine grace would mean, firstly to admit that the flow of divine grace from the Supreme Lord is not an eternal process but is in fact subject to fulfilling certain extraneous conditions. Secondly, it would come to conflict with the cardinal doctrine of Kashmir Tantric texts, viz *Svātantryavāda*.[18] Hence, the descent of divine grace must necessarily be regarded as an unconditional act of divine freedom (*ahetukī kṛpā*)[19] from the point of view of the Supreme Lord.

The Tantric theory about the quantitative difference in the intensity of divine grace, which is discernible only from the point of view of aspirants and not from the point of view of the Supreme Lord, was first postulated by the *Mālīnīvijayottara Tantra* but was later developed by Abhinavagupta in his *Tantrāloka*[20] and *Tantrasāra*.[21] This theory might appear something peculiar to the Śaiva Tāntrika stream of thought, but its parallel can be seen in the Vaiṣṇava theology and the Catholic religion, which also believe in the existence of intrinsic differences in men. The differences are not superficial but basic, ascribable to the subtle moment (*kṣaṇa*) of their creation or coming into existence. Thus, outwardly all men are similar in all respects and identical in essence, but, as a matter of fact, there are intrinsic differences in them, so much so that every individual has a distinct personality of his own. The Vaiṣṇava theologians speak of three kinds of *mukti* (liberation), viz *sāmīpya* (achievement of nearness to the Godhead), *sārūpya* (achievement of union with the Supreme God) and *svarūpya* (achievement of oneness with the Supreme God), which supports for innate differentiation in men. The Catholic theologians elaborated the Doctrine of the Elect in which they appear to subscribe to the same view.

---

17 *Ibid.*

18 M.V.T. IX, 37.

19 T.S., Ah. XI.

20 T.A. vol. VIII, Ah. XIII.

21 T.S. Ah. XI.

Guru (divine teacher) and his kinds

Related with the Tantric doctrine of divine grace is the Tantric conception of *guru*, who serves as the medium for the transmission of the divine grace to the individual beings. The *guru*, as an abstract principle in the field of Tantra Yoga, represents the Supreme Lord as the Supreme Compassion (*anugraha* or *kṛpā*) incarnate.[22] He not only serves as the medium for the flow of divine grace from the highest source, that is the Supreme Lord, but he also serves on the worldly level as the friend philosopher and guide to the aspirant in his spiritual journey to the ultimate Destiny. The divine grace, as a rule, cannot flow directly from the original source, i.e. the Supreme Lord, hence the need and importance of the *guru* as the relaying medium has been recognised in the Tantric texts.[23] He functions completely under the will (*icchā*) of the Supreme Lord, whom he represents on the lower level.

Generally speaking, he is an embodied being, but his body is not made of dominantly impure matter.[24] He is said to have his body completely purged of impure matter, such *mala* as the *āṇavamala* on account of his possessing divine enlightenment, which has been termed as the *jñāna cakṣu* or the 'eye of wisdom'. It is also known as the 'third eye' *(tṛtīya netra* or *prajñā cakṣu*), the possession of which enables him to 'open' the eyes of wisdom in his disciple through what has been generally termed as *jñānāñjana śalākā* (lit. instrument for removing by spiritual knowledge the darkness of ignorance prevailing in the disciple). The *guru* thus possesses the capacity, on account of his having enlightenment, to free the disciple from the web of ignorance through his own power and to elevate him to a higher spiritual level of existence so that he can feel himself free of the bondage arising out of the false identification of the self with the not-self (*dehātmabodha*).[25]

---

[22] Cf. T.S. XI p. 124 f.

[23] *Ibid.* [24] *Ibid.*

[25] Abhinavagupta distinguishes *sadguru* from *asadguru*. See T.S. XI, p. 12.

In this connection, it would not be perhaps out of place to mention that the individual beings in bondage are, in the Tantric view, subject to the operation of two mutually opposite currents of *śakti* ceaselessly functioning in their psycho-physical body through the inhalation and exhalation of breath, technically called *prāṇa* and *apāna*. The ceaseless functioning of these two vital airs, one of them dominating over the other at one time, is the root cause of all their misery and their existence in ignorance.[26] This has to be first controlled in gradual steps, and then finally stopped before the 'third eye' can be opened in them. It may be recalled here that the seers had recognised this long ago, and prescribed *prāṇāyāma* as a method to control the functioning of vital airs (*prāṇa vāyu*). Even Gautama Buddha, who promulgated the doctrine of the Middle Path (*madhyamamārga*), practised this form of Yoga, and therefore was probably influenced by it in postulating this doctrine. The *guru* shows his disciple the practical way to regulate the functioning of *prāṇa* and *apāna vāyu* so that a perfect equilibrium can be established between them, thus paving the way for the opening of the middle path (technically called *suṣumṇā*) for the ascent of the Primal Energy (technically called *Kuṇḍalinī śakti*) lying coiled up at the *mūlādhāra cakra*.[27] We shall discuss this in some detail in the succeeding chapter together with the role it plays in the realisation of one's true nature. This culminates in the opening of the 'third eye', which was closed heretofore. The *guru* simultaneously infuses his disciple with divine grace in an appropriate measure, commensurate with his capacity to receive it. The infusion of grace results in the rise of pure knowledge, technically called *sattarka* or *prātibha jñāna*,[28] which will be discussed separately later. The *guru* plays thus an important role, and it is for this reason that the Tantric texts unanimously acclaim his indispensability so far as spiritual discipline is concerned.

---

[26] Pr. Hd. Sū 14 com.

[27] Pr. Hd. Su 14.

[28] For its nature see T.S. IV, p. 21-23.

In this connection, it may be mentioned that certain Tantric texts like the *Mālinīvijayottara Tantra* make a distinction between a *sadguru* (real divine teacher) and a *guru* (teacher) or *asad-guru* (not-real teacher).[29] A *sadguru* is one who, having attained perfect union with the supreme Lord, is capable of leading one to the attainment of both enjoyment (*bhoga*) and liberation (*mukti*) all at once, besides the supreme knowledge or *sattarka*. An *asadguru*, on the other hand, is one who, having failed to achieve the supreme knowledge or *sattarka* directly as a consequence of his union with the Supreme Lord, acquires it from the secondary sources, such as study of *Āgamic* texts, or from his contact with a *sadguru*, etc.[30] Such *gurus* might succeed in arousing desire in other aspirants for achieving the Supreme Goal through their contact with them, but they are incapable of transmitting divine grace as they themselves have no contact with the Supreme Lord who is the real source of divine grace.[31] There are different kinds of *gurus*, such as *vidyā-guru* (teacher), *kulaguru* (family teacher), etc, who are too well known to be described here. The Tantric texts do not underrate the value of such *gurus* in the life of the ordinary individual as they also play a significant role in the initial stages,[32] but they do not attach much importance to them inso-far as spiritual discipline is concerned, being incapable of relaying the divine grace which alone plays a crucial role in the Tantra Yoga.

Broadly speaking, the Tantric texts mention four distinct types of *sadgurus* (real divine teachers), viz *akalpita guru*, *akalpitakālpaka guru*, *kalpita guru* and *kapitākalpita guru*.[33] The *akalpita gurus* are those in whom the supreme knowledge or *sattarka* rises without their having made any effort in whatsoever form, and therefore they do not have to undergo any such rites as *abhiṣeka* (annointing) or *dīksā* (initiation) by any external *guru*. Such persons are said to be groomed

---

[29] M.V.T. IV, p. 25; T.S. XI, p. 123.

[30] T.S. XI, p. 121.

[31] *Ibid.*, p. 124.

[32] M.V.T. IV, p. 25.

[33] Quoted by G.N. Kaviraj: *Tāntrika Sādhanā* etc., p. 80-83.

for this enviable position by the Supreme Lord Himself, hence they do not stand in need of any help from any other *guru*. They are therefore regarded as the highest class of *guru*, possessing the supreme enlightenment, also called *prātibhjñāna*, as an innate quality, whereby they are able to gain insight into the secrets of all the *Śāstras* and reality all around them without making effort.[34] Such fortunate few have nothing to achieve, as they are said to remain ever immersed in their divine *svarūpa* (nature). As *gurus* of the highest order, they are said to serve as a medium for transmission of the divine grace from the Supreme Lord. The Pātañjala Yoga speaks of Īśvara as the *sāṁsiddhika guru* whose main function is to dispense grace to individual souls in bondage.[35] He corresponds in fact to the *akalpita guru* of the Tantric tradition in nature, status and function.

The *akalpitākalpaka gurus* are also a high class of *gurus*, who are said to have the supreme enlightenment after having put in personal efforts in the form of *bhāvanā*, etc. Like the *akalpita gurus*, they are said to have the supreme enlightenment inherent in them, but this does not arise automatically.[36] They seem to suffer from some kind of deficiency for the removal of which they are required to take recourse to such measures as intense concentration (*bhāvanā*). Such *gurus* resemble the *akalpita* ones in as much as they do not stand in need of any help from an external *guru* other than the Supreme Lord himself, nor have to undergo purificatory rites such as *abhiṣeka*, etc.

The *kalpita gurus*[37] are a relatively inferior class of *gurus* who obtain the supreme enlightenment after receiving the divine grace through an external *guru* and undergoing such purificatory rites as *abhiṣeka* and *dīkṣā*. Such *gurus* have to make intense personal efforts to make their psycho-physical body-apparatus a suitable medium to act as *guru*. Being dependent on external factors, such as an external *guru*, *dīkṣā*, etc for the rise of supreme enlightenment in them, such persons obviously occupy lower position in the hierarchy of *gurus*.

---

[34] Cf. *aupadesikajnnana* mentioned in *Vyāsabhāṣya*.

[35] Cf. *Yoga Sūtra* I.

[36] See G.N. Kaviraj: *Tāntrika Sādhanā. Siddhānta* Part I. p. 80-83.

[37] *Ibid.*

The *kalpitakalpaka gurus* are those who are said to depend on such external factors as a *guru* other than the Supreme Lord, and undergo such rites as *abhiṣeka* and *dīkṣā* like the *kalpita* ones, but they generally obtain the supreme enlightenment in its full splendour through their personal efforts. Thus the rise of the supreme enlightenment in their case is believed to be more or less independent of external factors (*akalpita*) unlike in the case of *kalpita gurus*; such *gurus* are technically called *kalpita-akalpaka*. It may be mentioned here that such kind of *gurus* are very rare.

Looking from another point of view, some Tantric texts have broadly classified them under three heads, viz *daiva guru* or celestial teachers, *siddha guru* or superhuman teachers and *puruṣa guru* or human teachers.

The *daiva guru* or celestial teachers are those teachers who dispense the divine grace to the superior-most kind of aspirants, attaining the highest degree of perfection through their personal efforts by dissociating themselves completely from matter through discriminatory wisdom (*vivekajñāna*). The *Mālinīvijayottara Tantra* mentions the presiding deities (*ādhikārika devatās*) of different regions such as *Rudra, Brahmā, Viṣṇu, Mantramaneśvara, mantra*[38] etc. as examples of celestial teachers. It has been mentioned that any individual *sādhaka* who possessed an innate desire for enjoyment (*bhogavāsanā*) and had succeeded through his intense personal efforts in dissociating himself completely from impure matter, could attain the elevated position of an *ādhikārika devatā* (presiding deity), after receiving the divine grace in an appropriate intense measure and act as a celestial teacher (*daiva guru*). Such celestial teachers, as a rule, possess a body made of pure matter, technically called *baindava deha*, as they stay on the levels above *Māyā*, that is the region of *Mahāmāyā* or *śuddha adhva* (pure order).

The *siddha* teachers are perfect embodied beings who occupy elevated positions compared to ordinary human aspirants owing to

[38] *Ibid.*, p. 83.

their possessing a pure psycho-physical body-apparatus and their intimate connection with the Supreme Lord. Here mention may be made of four kinds of *yogins* admitted by the Tantric texts, viz *samprāpta yogins*, *ghaṭamāna yogins*, *siddha yogins* and *susiddha yogins*.[39] Those *yogins* who have received instructions on yoga are called *samprāpta yogins*, while those who have started practising discipline in accordance with the yogic instructions are known as *ghaṭamāna yogins*.[40] Obviously, these two categories of *yogins* are incapable of rendering help to other aspirants as they themselves are said to have just embarked on the path of Tantra Yoga. The *siddha yogins*[41] are those who have not only attained the supreme enlightenment but are capable of giving a glimpse of it to other aspirants, and thus serve as the instrument of the will (*icchā*) of the Supreme Lord in so far as dispensing of divine grace is concerned. The *siddha* teachers in fact belong to this category of *yogins*. The *susiddha yogins*[42] are the highest type of *yogins*; having obtained a firm establishment in the state of supreme enlightenment, they always remain in that state. They are said to have crossed all levels of existence, and hence are believed to stay above the ordinary levels of existence, They are also said to possess the capacity to act as *guru*, but they are generally not available to ordinary aspirants.[43] In fact it is said that they function as *gurus* only through the *vidyeśvaras*.

The *puruṣa gurus* (teachers in human form) are those embodied human *gurus* who apparently exist on the superior plane as the human disciples, but they in fact occupy a superior position owing to their possessing a pure body-apparatus or *ādhāra* and their intimate connection with the Supreme Lord whom they serve as instruments of divine *anugraha*. A large number of aspirants are associated with impure matter, hence they are ordinarily incapable of approaching *gurus* belonging to the higher levels of existence. They, therefore, have to depend on human *gurus* for receiving divine grace through them.

---

39 T.S. XI p. 118.

40 M.V.T. IV, 33 p. 25.

41 *Ibid.*, IV, 35-36 p. 25.

42 *Ibid.*, IV, 37 p. 25.

43 M.V.T., IV, 38 p. 26.

All the Tantric texts, irrespective of the stream of thought to which they belong, declare that the Supreme Lord is the highest *guru*, the source of divine grace. As has already been stated, the performance of the five eternal functions is His unique characteristic.[44] Of these functions, *anugraha* (dispensation of divine grace) is the principal one, which He does directly or through some medium considered to be His own instrument. The Supreme Lord pervades everywhere by virtue of His omnipresence. He occupies every position simultaneously, without abjuring His transcendent Nature. He can adopt any medium of His own choice for transmitting the divine grace who, at that moment, comes to be known as the *guru* to that particular individual. The elevation of a human individual is generally temporary, as it last till the exhaustion of the residual impressions of his meritorious deeds, when he retires giving place to another human individual who continues the function and thus keeps the chain unbroken.

[44] *Ibid.*, IV, 36 p. 26.

~Chapter VII~

Dīkṣā (Initiation)

Dīkṣā, its meaning and role in spiritual discipline

After the descent of divine grace from the highest Source, i.e. the Supreme Lord, through the medium of the *guru*, *dīkṣā* (initiation) is the most important step towards the achievement of the Supreme. It has been defined as that "step where the supreme knowledge is imparted and the fetters are cut asunder".[1] Supreme Knowledge, which has been technically called *pauruṣa jnāna*[2] in the Śaiva Tantras, lies dormant within every individual so long as the different *malas* acting as sheaths exist in him. Supreme knowledge does not lie on the plane of the intellect, and therefore, has been described as of a non-conceptual nature (*vaikalpika*).[3] As such, it cannot coexist with the ego-sense (*ahaṁkāra*), which is conceptual by nature, and therefore not true. It is however said to be of the nature of *pūrṇāhaṁtā* (supreme Self-experience), which is characterised by the manifestation of the *svātantrya* (divine Freedom).[4] The manifestation of *pūrṇāhaṁtā* in the individual is not possible till all his fetters are not destroyed, fetters that exist in him ever since the first creation in the form of three *malas*, viz *āṇava*, *māyīya* and *kārma*. This is exactly what is achieved by *dīkṣā*, the most important step in the individual's spiritual life. The two impediments in the path leading to the achievement of the *summum bonum* are in particular the two *malas*, *āṇava mala*

---

[1] *Dīyate jñāna sadbhāvāh, kṣīyate paśuvāsanā |*
dāhakṣapaṇa-samyuktā dīkṣā teneh kīrtitā ||

[2] Cf. T.S. A.I., p. 2-3.

[3] *Ibid.*

[4] See author's article, in 'Corpus of Indian Studies', Calcutta, 1980, p. 153-64.

(fundamental defilement in the form of self-contraction) and *kārma*, which corresponds to the *prārabdha karma* of the orthodox schools of Indian philosophy and therefore responsible for the continuance of the embodied state.[5] The process of Tantric initiation eradicates these two *malas*, paving the way for the rise of *pauruṣa jñāna*, which laid concealed theretofore in the individual.

Kinds of *dīkṣā*

The process of initiation differs from individual to individual, depending on the degree of intensity of divine grace received by every individual. Broadly speaking, there are four kinds of *dīkṣā*, viz *anupāyadīkṣā*, *śāṁbhavī dīkṣā*, *śakti dīkṣā* and *āṇavī dīkṣā*, in accordance with the descent of divine grace on the individual in most intense, more intense, intense and mild forms. The *anupāya dīkṣā* is the highest kind of *dīkṣā*, available only to those who have received the divine grace in its most intense form. This *dīkṣā* is so powerful that it enables the aspirant to realise the supreme Goal almost instantaneously,[6] without entailing any effort on the part of the individual.

The *śāmbhavi dīkṣā*, which also is only available to a fortunate few, results too in the realisation of their ultimate Destiny, namely *Śivatva*, almost instantaneously, though the *sādhaka* has to pass through certain states of mystic experience when they are said to intuitively 'see' in their pure *citta* (*cidākāśā*) the ever-vibrating divine Śakti in its fullness as the supreme Light.[7] The different phases of Śakti, technically called *kalās*, symbolised by the different *varṇas* (letters), gradually unfold themselves in his experience, which, later, coalesce in his Self experience as *Aham*.[8] This mystic self-experience

[5] The *kārmamala* has been held responsible for one's birth (i.e. association with a body), *āyu* (the period of one's association with body) and *bhoga* (enjoyment). It is also said to produce the sheet in the form of five *kañcukas*. See I.P.V. III, 2, 45, p. 244.

[6] T.S. II, p. 8-9.

[7] *Ibid.*, III, p. 10-12.

[8] T.S., p. 10-16.

of *Aham* contains within it the infinite variety in the play of the divine Śakti, as a result of which the creation is 'unfolded' (*unmiṣati*) without. The aspirant then experiences that the entire range of creation, resulting from the play of the divine Śakti, as nothing but an extension of his divine nature as Śiva (the Lord), as a self-projection. Thus the aspirant realises his divinity in its full glory, which is the supreme Goal.[9]

The *śakti-dīkṣā*, though equally powerful in the removal of the veil of ignorance from the intellect, fails in removing the veil from *buddhi*. As a result of this, this false experience of self in the not-self (*anātmani-ātmabodha*), technically called *aśuddha vikalpa,* persists. The individual aspirant is required to make special efforts for its removal through transformation or purification (*saṁskāra*) of *aśuddha vikalpa* through a process technically called *bhāvanā saṁskāra*.[10] In this task, *sattarka* or *prātibha jñāna* (pure intuitive knowledge) plays an important role. It is believed that the *sattarka* or *prātibhajñāna* arises automatically in the aspirant's *buddhi* (intellect) with the descent of divine grace and the accomplishment of *dīkṣā*, but if the *buddhi* continues to remain clouded by the persisting veil of ignorance due to the mildness of grace, the aspirant then is required to take recourse to such instruments as the study of *sadāgama* (appropriate) Āgamic texts) or listen to the spiritual discourses given by the *guru* (*gurūpadeśa*).[11] Even the performance of *dhyāna* (concentration), *yoga*, *japa* (repetition of sacred *mantras*), *vrata* (austerities), *homa* (sacrifice) in the manner laid down in the *Āgamas* might be necessary for cleansing the intellect and transforming the *aśuddha vikalpa* into *śuddha vikalpa* (pure knowledge in the form of the experience of self in the Self).[12]

The *āṇavi dīkṣā* is generally given to those who are recipient of divine grace in a very mild form. The mildness of grace received by

---

[9] *Ibid.*, p. 18-19.

[10] *Ibid.*, IV, pp. 21-22.

[11] *Ibid.*, pp. 26-27.

[12] T.S.

the aspirant results in the persistence of the veil of ignorance in the intellect in the form of a thick layer, which cannot be removed by ordinary means. Such *sādhakas* are, therefore, required to resort to *Kriyā Yoga*[13] in the manner prescribed by the Tantric texts. It has been said that the aspirants have to take help from such supports (*ālambanas*) as *prāṇaśakti*, *buddhi*, physical body, etc,[14] for their progress in the spiritual path as directed by the *guru* at the time of their initiation (*dīkṣā*). In this connection it might be mentioned here that the *Saḍanvayamahāratna* mentions ten kinds of *āṇavī dīkṣā*,[15] which are briefly described below:

(i) *Smārti āṇavi-dīkṣā* — The *guru* sometimes destroys the three kinds of *pāśas* in the body of his disciple, who happens to be staying at a distance, by establishing contact with him through remembrance (*smaraṇa*). Thereafter he directs him to perform *laya yoga*.

(ii) *Mānasi-aṇavī dīkṣā* — The *guru* generally makes the disciple sit near him and destroys the three kinds of *pāśas* (fetters) existing in his *ādhāra* (i.e. body) through mental communion.

(iii) *Yaugī-āṇavī dīkṣā* — The *guru* enters into the body of his disciple through a yogic method and establishes identity with him while performing this kind of *dīkṣā*.

(iv) *Cākṣuṣī-āṇavī dīkṣā* — The *guru* sometimes casts a glance on his disciple while in trance, and thus performs this kind of *dīkṣā*.

(v) *Sparśinī-āṇavī dīkṣā* — The *guru* sometimes touches the head of his disciple with his hand, muttering appropriate *mantras*, and thus performs this kind of *dīksā*.

(vi) *Vācaki-āṇavī dīkṣā* — In this kind of *dīkṣā* the *guru* tells his disciple the holy *mantras*, showing him the way *mudrā*, *nyāsa*, etc. are to be performed. The disciple is required to repeat the holy *mantras* along with the *mudrānyāsa* daily in order to cleanse his body and thereafter achieve the supreme Goal.

---

13 *Ibid.*, V, p. 35.

14 *Ibid.*

15 Cf. G.N. Kaviraj: *Tāntrik Sādhanā. Siddhānta*, *Ibid.*, I, p. 215.

(vii) *Māntrikī-āṇavī dīkṣā* — The *guru* sometimes 'delivers' the holy *mantra* to his disciple by becoming an embodiment of the *mantra* itself. He accomplishes this along with *mantranyāsa*.

It may be mentioned here that *cākṣuṣī*, *sparśinī*, *vācikī* and *māntrikī ānavi dikṣās* are very popular forms of *āṇavī dīkṣā* that are performed sometimes.[16]

(viii) *Hautri-āṇavī-dīksā* — The *guru* sometimes performs *homa* (sacrifice) for the purification of various kinds of *adhvas* in the disciple, and thus performs this kind of *dīkśā*.

(ix) *Śāstrī-āṇavī-dīksā* — The *guru* sometimes teaches the duly qualified disciple the real meaning of the Āgamic texts. Obviously, for this kind of *dīksā*, the disciple must possess appropriate mental qualities and must have full faith in the truth revealed by the *Āgamas*.

(x) *Abhiśecakī-āṇavī-dīksā* — The *guru* performs this kind of *dīkśā* by propitiating Śiva and Śakti in a pitcher in the prescribed manner. This is also called *Śivakumbhābhiṣeka dīksā*.[17]

There is yet another classification of *dīkṣā* mentioned in some Tantric texts[18] from a different point of view. It is said to be of eight kinds, as mentioned by Abhinavagupta. These are *samaya dīkśā*, *putraka dīkśā*, *śivadharminī dīkśā*, *lokadharmiṇī dikṣā*, *kriyā dikṣā*, *jñāna dīkṣā*, *sabīja dīkṣā* and *nirbīja dīkṣā*. There is a sort of gradation in these different types of *dīkṣā*, as they are in some cases complementary to each other, leading one to the achievement of different goals. For instance, *samayadīkṣā*, the preliminary *dīkṣā*, available to all those aspirants in whom the *malas* have ripened under the influence of *kālaśakti* (power of time)[19] and who have received the divine grace

---

[16] G.N. Kaviraj in his *Tāntric Sādhānā O Sidddhānta*, p. 215.

[17] *Tāntric Sādhānā O Sidddhānta*, p. 215.

[18] See *Svacchanda Tantra* II. p. 241 ff. for various kinds of *dīkśā*.

[19] The *kālaśakti*, also called *raudriśakti* of *kalāgnirudra* is nothing but a form of the *kriyā śakti* of the Supreme Lord. It is said that due to the incessant functioning of the *kriyā śakti* of the Supreme Lord, the *malas* in all the fettered beings undergo maturation in cause of time. The *dikṣā* itself is an aspect of the *raudrī kriyā śaktī*.

in mild form. The *guru* appears at the right moment to place his hand, technically called *Śivahasta*, on the head of the disciple and thereafter initiate him into the secrets of *Āgama Śāstra*. Thereafter, the disciple becomes qualified for performing various forms of *kriyā* such as *homa* (sacrifice), *japa* (repetition of sacred *mantras*), *pujā* (worship), *dhyāna* (meditation), etc, as prescribed in the Āgamic texts. It has been said that the task of the purification of the disciple is accomplished by *samayācāra*,[20] consisting of *caryā* and *dhyāna*. The carrying out of rites prescribed by the *Āgamas* on the lines indicated by the *guru* is called *caryā*. *Dhyāna* signifies control of breath, etc, and meditation as laid down in the *Āgamas*. It is true that this kind of *dīkṣā* does not end in the achievement of the ultimate goal but it is capable of leading one to the achievement of the status of *Īśvara* or lower kind of *mukti* (liberation) and also enables one to receive a higher kind of *dīkṣā*, such as *putraka*, etc. One of the purposes of *sāmayī dīkṣā* is the purification of different kinds of *pāśas* (fetters) in the *paśu* (fettered beings, i.e. men in bondage), but this purification does not necessarily result in their destruction. In fact, the purification of *pāśas* leads one to the achievement of some of the divine powers of the Lord, whose proximity he achieves through his efforts.

Broadly speaking, the *sāmayī dīkṣā* brings about the purification in three steps, viz *jatyuddhāra* (achievement of one's elevation from his present level of existence in embodied beings), *dvijatvaprāpti*[21] (achievement of the status of 'twice-born'), *rudrāṁśaprāpti* (achievement of the touch with the Divine). The moment the *guru* places his *Śivahasta* on the head of the disciple, the process of transformation sets in his psychophysical body.[22] Prior to his receiving the *sāmayī dīkṣā*, his physical body was the resultant of his *prārabdha karma* (the ripened *kārmic* seeds yielding result), hence it was incapable of performing *sādhanā* on the lines as laid down in the *Āgamas*. The performance of *sāmayī dīkṣā* sets in motion the process of trans-

---

[20] Cf. MVT, VIII, pp. 40-46.

[21] M.V.T. VIII, 131.

[22] *Ibid.*, IX, 44.

formation of all the constituent elements in his body, from impure physical to pure physical, which, in fact, is the resultant of the sacred *mantra* given to the disciple by the *guru* at the time of his initiation.[23] The *mantra* given to the disciple is not merely a combination of certain sounds (*varṇa*), it symbolises the divine Śakti that has been 'aroused' by the *guru* in the form of *mantra* and given to the disciple. As he repeats the sacred *mantra*, it acts from within, bringing about in gradual steps a total change in his body-apparatus. When the body-apparatus of the disciple becomes completely purified through the *mantra*[24] the disciple attains *dvijatva* (the state of twice-born). It may be mentioned here that the various *Gṛhyasūtras* and *Smṛtis* prescribe forty *saṁskāras*, beginning with *garbhādhāna* (causing impregnation), as a result of which a person is said to become a *dvija* (twice-born). The *Āgamas* accept these *sāṁskāras* as a means to attain *dvijatva* (the status of twice-born), but add that if these *saṁskāras* are performed along with the use of certain *mantras* laid down in the *Āgamas* under the supervision of a *guru*, one can become a *dvija* of the highest order. The entire process leading to the attainment of *dvijatva* is thus, in the eyes of the *Āgamas*, essentially a spiritual process of transformation of one's body-apparatus as against the one laid down in the texts of *Dharmaśāstra* which aims at the purification (*saṁskāra*) on the physical level only. Hence it is said that, following the performance of *sāmayīdīkṣā* and the consequent transformation of the body-apparatus of the disciples under *jātyuddhāra*, they attain only one kind of *dvijatva*,[25] viz. *śivamayī* or *bhairavī dvijatva*, as against three different kinds of *dvijatva* following the *saṁskāras* as laid down in the *Dharmaśāstras*.

The next step is *rudrāṁśaprāpti*, i.e. attainment of contact with the Divine whereby one ultimately becomes the Divine. It has been said that the *guru* should first perform the *prokṣaṇa kriyā* (sprinkling)

---

[23] T.S., IX, 49-50.

[24] T.S. XII, p. 130.

[25] G.N. Kaviraj: *Tāntrik Sādhanā O Siddhānta*, p. 216. Also see *Svacchanda Tantra*.

and the *tāḍanā kriyā*[26] (striking) in the body-apparatus of his disciple at the very outset. Thereafter he should 'take himself out' of his own body through *recaka kriyā* (process of going out), and enter into the body of his disciple and 'rise up' to the level of his 'head' (the central place) in order to slacken his disciple's intimate connection with his gross physical body (*sthūla śarīra* or *puryaṣaṭaka*). This entire process is technically called *viśleṣana kriyā* (the process of slackening).[27] Then the *guru* should cover the 'bond of connection' between the self and the body in the disciple's body and thereafter raise it to bring on the level of *dvādaśānta* or the head. Then he should draw his disciple up after 'closing him up' on the lines of a lotus flower through *saṁhāra mudrā*. While accomplishing all these tasks in the body of his disciple, the *guru* should keep himself identified with his disciple in his body. Thereafter, he should 'return' to his own body through a process called *ūrdhvarecaka*.[28]

As the disciple 'rises up' or soars on being pulled up by his *guru* acting within his body, he passes through six steps on which he is said to 'abandon', six *devatās* (the presiding deities) stationed on different levels within his body as well as outside his body. These are: Brahmā on the level of 'heart', Viṣṇu on the 'throat' (*kaṇṭha*), Rudra on the *tālu* (palate), Īśvara on the space between the two eyebrows (*bhrūmadhya*), Śadāśiva on the forehead (*lalāṭa*) and Śiva on the *brahmarandhra*.[29] The journey of the disciple within his body as a result of his being pulled up by the *guru* from within, simultaneously results his crossing the six levels of existence on the outer plane in the external world, technically called *ṣaḍadhva*[30]. This also endows him with the capacity for the worship of the Supreme Lord through whose grace he ultimately succeeds in attaining the status of Īśvara.

---

[26] Cf. M.V.T. IX, 58.

[27] *Ibid.*, IX, 49.

[28] T.S.. XIII, p. 41.

[29] MVT IX, p. 51.

[30] *Ibid.*, IX, p. 53-54.

Sāmayī dīkṣā is generally followed by *putraka dīkṣa*,[31] though in exceptional cases the latter is not preceded by the former. *Putraka dīkṣā* cannot take place without the purification of the six *adhvas* having been accomplished beforehand, which also involves the purification of *pāśas*, hence *sāmayī dīkṣā* is said to precede the *putraka dīkṣā*. This is because *putraka dīkṣā* involves the *sādhaka*'s coming in contact with the Supreme Being, which is impossible without the eradication of *malas*. The *sāmayī dīkṣā* not only results in establishing a short relationship of the *sādhaka* with the Supreme Being, it is also said to accomplish, though partially in the initial stage, the destruction of *pāśas*, hence it has been assigned the first place among the different types of *dīkṣās*. In some cases, where the divine grace has been received by the *sādhaka* in a sufficiently intense form, the destruction of *pāśas* is accomplished simultaneously by the divine grace itself, hence in such cases the *putraka dīkṣā* can take place directly without being preceded by *sāmayī dīkṣā*. It has been enjoined that the *guru*, while performing the *putraka dīkṣā*, should first see the inclination of his disciple. For, broadly speaking, there are two kinds of *sādhakas* — some aspire for pure enjoyment on the higher spiritual planes, while others consider the attainment of emancipation to be their supreme goal.[32] It has been laid down that the *guru* should not destroy the residual impressions of meritorious deeds (*śubha karma saṁkāras*) lying in his *ādhāra* (i.e. the psycho-physical body), in order to enable him to continue to live in an embodied condition to enjoy pure *bhoga*,[33] after attaining a divine status through his contact with the divine Being. The *sādhakas* who desire emancipation are of two kinds: some are inclined toward striving for their own emancipation, and others depend wholly on the *guru* for help. The *guru* should bear in mind this distinction before administering this kind of *dīkṣā*, which eradicates all kinds of *pāśas* that the *sādhakas* may have. A detailed description of the rites performed at the time of

---

[31] T.S. XIV, p. 156.

[32] Cf. T.S. XIV, 158; Also see M.V.T. XI, 1.

[33] Cf. *Bhogecchoḥ śubham na śodhayet*. Ibid.

this *dīkṣā* has been given in *Āgama* texts like the *Mālinījayottara Tantra*, which has been summarised by Abhinavagupta in his *magnum opus*, *Tantrāloka*, and his smaller text, *Tantrasāra* (Ahn. XIV).

Some *Āgama* texts mention two distinct types of *sādhakas* among those who desire to have pure enjoyment on the higher spiritual planes. They are technically called *śivadharmiṇī sādhakas* and *lokadharmiṇī sādhakas*,[34] and accordingly two different kinds of *dīkṣā* named after these *sādhaka* types are administered to them by the *guru*. As a result of *śivadharminī dīkṣa*, the *sādhakas* achieve three different kinds of *siddhis* in accordance with their capacity, such as the attainment of the status of *Mantreśvara*, or *Mantra*, or the achievement of *piṇḍa-siddhi*, i.e. perfection of their body-apparatus.[35] The attainment of the status of *Mantreśvara* or *Mantra* by the *sādhakas* not only results in their elevation to the higher levels of pure beings (*ādhikārika devatā*), it also provides them with the opportunity to govern on the different regions under them.

The attainment of *piṇḍasiddhi* confers on them certain opportunities for pure *bhoga* on the level where they happen to exist. The *sādhakas* enjoy the fruit, almost equivalent to the upaniṣadic *amṛtattva* (lit. immortality),[36] after having attained bodies free from all kinds of mutation, such as old age, death, etc. Such bodies are not destroyed even at the time of the cosmic dissolution (*pralaya*); hence they continue to exist as Enlightened Beings till they desire to achieve *Śivatva*. Other kinds of *siddhis* mentioned in the *Mālinīvijayottara Tantra*, such as *khaḍgasiddhi*, *pādukāsiddhi* (whereby they are able to move through air at will), *añjanasiddhi*, etc, are also included in this category.[37] The *śivadharmīṇī dikṣā* is available to both *saṁnyāsins* who have renounced this world and *gṛhastas*, i.e. those who continue to lead a family life.

---

[34] Cf. *Svacchanda Tantra* II, 141-144.

[35] *Ibid*., T. 144.

[36] Cf. *Kaṭhopanisad*. See author's article "Kaṭhopaniṣad varṇita tīna varon kā ādhyatmika mahattva" in *Viśva Jyoti*. Upaniṣadaṅka. Hoshiarpur.

[37] Cf. M.V.T. XIII, p. 84 ff.

The *sādhakas* eligible for the *lokadharmiṇī dīkṣā* are those who desire their union with the Supreme Being, the Supreme Lord.[38] It has been said that when the *guru* gives this kind of *dīkṣā*, the residual impressions of demeritorious *karmas* (*pāpa*) of the past as well as of the future are destroyed, but the residual impressions of the meritorious *karmas* performed by the *sādhaka* in the past continue to exist, which later are converted into various kinds of *siddhis* such as *aṇimā*, *laghimā, prāpti*, etc, as found described in the Pātañjala Yoga system. The residual impressions of past *karmas* which have begun to fructify, technically called *prārabdha karma*, are however not affected by this kind of *dīkṣā*, and therefore the *sādhaka* has to exhaust them through enjoyment (*bhoga*). It has been said down that if the *guru* finds in the *sādhaka* the desire to lurk for the pure *bhoga* of various kinds of *siddhis*, he should send him to higher levels of existence after his dissociation from the gross physical body caused by exhaustion of the fruits of *prārabdha karma*, from where he ultimately attains union with the Supreme Lord. In rare cases, where the *sādhakas* desire for union with the presiding deities of regions beyond *Māyā*, the *guru* unites them with these deities after initiating them accordingly.

The *sādhakas* who aspire for the attainment of personal liberation, which in fact means union with the Supreme Lord, can be put under three categories[39] — first are those who are not endowed with the adequate mental perfection and hence are incapable of understanding the true significance of the supreme Truth. The immature young persons, the grown up but mentally deficient persons, the old and infirm, ladies, etc, come under this categories for whom *nirbīja dīkṣā* has been prescribed. It has been said in the *Svacchanda Tantra* that such *sādhakas* attain liberation directly as a result of this kind of *dīkṣā* as they possess a pure *ādhāra* and have *bhakti* (devotion) towards the *guru*.[40] Such *sādhakas* do not have to follow *samayācāra* as laid down in the *Āgamic* texts.

---

[38] *Svach Ta*. II, 141.

[39] Svac. Tan II, 453.

[40] Cf. *ibid*.

In the case of some *sādhakas* who are ill and about to die, and are thus incapable of performing the arduous task of *sādhanā*, it has been laid down that the *guru* should perform in such base *sadyo-nirvāṇadāyinī dīkṣā*, i.e. a *dīkṣā* which is capable of bringing the desired results instantaneously.[41] In such cases, the *guru* uses extremely powerful *mantras*, which are capable of purifying the *ādhāra* simultaneously with the *dīkṣā*. In the case of *sādhakas* who are extremely old or ill, it has been enjoined that the *guru* should 'draw them out' of their body and establish his union with the Supreme Lord.[42]

The *sādhakas* who possess intelligence and an adequate capacity for undertaking arduous spiritual discipline come under the third category of *sādhakas*. For them, *sabīja dīkṣā* has been prescribed. It has been laid down that *sabīja dīkṣā*[43] should be given to all those aspirants who have the innate capacity to occupy the position of *guru*, as this alone is capable to accomplish a direct contact with the Supreme Lord in absolute form. It has been said that *sabīja dīkṣā* should be given after performing the 'anointing ceremony' of the *sādhakas*. A detailed description of the anointing ceremony, technically called *abhiṣeka*,[44] has been given in the *Mālinīvijayottara Tantra*.

It has been laid down that the anointing ceremony of the disciple should be performed by placing five *kalaśas* (pitchers) round him in five quarters, namely South, North, West-east, and Iśāna *koṇa*. The five *kalās*, viz *nivṛtti*, *pratiṣṭhā*, *vidyā*, *śāntā* and *sāntyātītā*, representing respectively the group of *tattvas* beginning with *jala* up to *prakṛti*,[45] from *puruṣa* up to *śuddhavidyā*, from *śuddhavidyā* to *śakti tattva* and *śivatattva* are to be consecrated, one by one, on the five pitchers after uttering the appropriate *mantras* under the guidance of the *guru*. As the consecration is performed by the *guru*, the *sādhaka*

---

[41] T.S. XV pp. 68f.

[42] *Ibid.*

[43] Svach. Tan II, 146f.

[44] Op. cit., X pp. 68f.

[45] *Ibid.*

is elevated in gradual steps on the different levels of *tattvas* which are being consecrated, ending the rise up to the level of *śāntyātīta kalā*, i.e. *śivatattva*. When the disciple rises up to this level as a result of consecration, he attains a status similar to the Supreme Lord; hence he is able to enjoy the yogic powers or *siddhis*.[46]

A different kind of anointing ceremony for those who have the innate capacity to occupy the exalted position of *guru* has been prescribed.[47] This is because such *sādhakas* possess a pure *ādhāra* (body), and have certain moral virtues and qualities of intellect. It has been enjoined that this kind of anointing ceremony should be performed after initiation, which involves a direct connection of the disciple with the Supreme Being, technically called *Śivatvayojana* (lit. joining with the Supreme Being). Under this ceremony, when five pitchers are consecrated, symbolising the five *tattvas* and five *kalās* mentioned above, the five lords presiding over the different *bhuvanas* (regions), beginning with Ānanda and rising up to Śiva, have to be concentrated upon as stationed in the five pitchers.[48] Thereafter, the Supreme Lord is concentrated upon, uttering the prescribed *mantras*. Then a wooden (preferably of sandalwood) seat has to be placed in the centre of a specially drawn *maṇḍala* (figure prescribed in the *Āgamas*) under a canopy adorned with holy signs like *svastika*, etc. Near it, a flag has to be hoisted. After the disciple has been properly 'purified' through certain prescribed *saṁskāras* (purificatory rites), he is made to sit on the seat, where the *guru* worships him with flowers, etc, after being united with the supreme Lord. Thereafter the *āratī* of the disciple is performed, which is followed by pouring of holy waters from the pitcher, symbolising the *nivṛttikalā*. This ceremony is technically called *abhisecana* (bathing).[49] Then the disciple is made to discard his old clothes and put on new clothes, a ceremony which symbolises his discarding *Māyā* and its

---

[46] For details see *Tantra Sāra* An. X, p. 109f.

[47] Svacch. Tan. II, 141.

[48] Cf. G.N. Kaviraj: *Tāntrik Sādhanā O Siddhānta*, pp. 177 ff.

[49] Cf. T.S. XII, p. 129.

five *kañcukas* and putting on a new divine garb. After this ceremonial change of dress, the *guru* ordains him into the new order of *gurus* by giving him appropriate dresses such as head gear, *mukuṭa* (crown), umbrella, etc. He also utters the order of the Supreme thus: "Hereafter you are authorised to initiate those who are recipients of the divine grace in obedience to the divine Will". Thereafter, he should burn the five pitchers in fire, one by one, and touch the hand of the disciple with five fingers. This results in the manifestation of the *mantra śakti* as the divine 'glow', and all the *pāśas* of the disciple burn out instantaneously, as it were. The disciple then makes obeisance to the Supreme Lord, the *guru* and the burning *agni,* and attains both *jīvanmukti* (liberation while in body) as well as the *summum bonum*. At the same time, he is also endowed with the capacity of showing the spiritual path to others in deference to the divine will.

In addition to these different kinds of *dīkṣā*, the *Āgamas* mention two more varieties of *dīkṣā*, viz *jñāna dīkṣā* and *kriyā dīkṣā*.[50] The *jñāna dīkṣā* is that in which the *guru* not only initiates the disciple into the mysteries of spiritual discipline, which is characterised by supreme knowledge, but he also 'opens up' the knot of ignorance. It is the same for all aspirants. The *kriyā dīkṣā*, which involves taking help from *kriyā śakti* while performing the spiritual discipline, is of several kinds, depending on the *adhvas* or orders which one has to adopt and later cross, e.g. *kalādīkṣā*, *tattvadīkṣā*, *bhuvana dīkṣā*, *varṇa dīkṣā*, *mantra dīkṣā*, etc. The *tattvadīkṣā* again is of four kinds, viz *navatattva dīkṣa*, which involves the formation of 36 *tattvas* in nine such group as *prakṛti*, *puruṣa*, *niyatī*, *kalā*, *mayā*, *vidyā*, *Īśvara* and *Śiva*; or 5 *tattvas*, viz *pṛthvi, apas*, *tejas*, etc; or three *tattvas*, viz *Śiva*, *Māyā*, and *Ātmā*. The aim however is to realise the one *tattva*, viz *Bindu* (Potential Point), after merging all the *tattvas*. Here it may mentioned that Abhinavagupta in his *Tantrāloka* has mentioned at one place 74 kinds of *dīkṣā*, and at another he observes that *dīkṣā* is of an infinite variety, in keeping with the varying needs of the numerous disciples.[51]

[50] G.N. Kaviraj: *Tāntrik Sādhanā O Siddhānta*, p. 180.

[51] Cf. *anantabhāvānaśca dīkṣānantā vibheda-bhāk* | *Tantrasāra*.

The *Āgamas* are replete with accounts of various rites which follow *dīkṣā*, such as *adhva śodhana* (the purification of various *adhvas*), *kalā śodhana* (the purification of various *kalās*), *tattva śodhana* (the purification of *tattvas*), *varṇa śodhana* (the purification of various *varṇas* existing in the difference parts of one's body, which symbolises the universe), *homa* (sacrifice), *pūjā* (worship), all of which are symbolic acts of great esoteric content. The aim of all these rites is to make the disciple sever worldly ties, and have him ascend to higher levels of spiritual existence. As the true significance of all these rites is revealed by the *guru* to his disciple at the time of initiation, which are otherwise secret, we refrain from describing them here.

~CHAPTER VIII~

Nature and Role of Mantra in Spiritual Practices in the Tāntrika Tradition

We have seen in the foregoing pages that *dīkṣā* (initiation) is defined in the Tantric tradition as that particular rite in the spiritual life of a seeker of Truth in which the 'spiritual knowledge' (*jñāna*) is 'given' (*dīyate*), i.e. aroused by the spiritual master or *guru* in the disciple during initiation, resulting in the destruction of the fetters (*pāśa*) binding him (*kṣīyate paśuvāsanā*) to worldly life. We have discussed in that context the nature of the various kinds of fetters (*pāśa*) or defilements (*mala*) enveloping all embodied beings, thereby concealing their divine essence and making them forget their true nature. We have also shown how the infusion of divine grace (*anugraha* or *śaktipāta*) in a fettered spiritual seeker marks on one hand the beginning of the process of destruction of fetters in him in gradual steps, and on the other the revelation to him of his divine essence. The rationale for holding this view has also been explained in metaphysical terms as projected by the Advaita Śaivites in that context.

It is now proposed here to explain the implication of the expression 'spiritual knowledge' (*jñāna*) that the spiritual teacher is said to 'implant' in seed form in the intellect of the disciple in the form of *mantra* (sacred word) during his initiation (*dīkṣā*). We are going to describe in the following paragraphs the nature and different kinds of *mantras* that we come across in our daily as well as spiritual life, the manner the 'implanted' *mantra* is used by the disciple in his spiritual practices as directed by the *guru*, culminating in the revelation of the supreme integral knowledge (*akhaṇḍajñāna*) and illumining his intellect.

Meaning of the term '*mantra*'

Yāska in his *Nirukta* (etymological dictionary of Vedic words) has provided us with the etymological meaning of the term *mantra* in this way — *mantra* signifies that which saves one from taking recourse to reflection (*manana*), a kind of intellectual activity (*mananāt trāṇatā*). Abhinavagupta, while shedding light on the meaning of the word *mantra* from the point of view of Kashmir Śaivism, has accepted this etymological meaning given by Yāska. Śabara in his commentary of the *Mīmāṁsā Sūtra* of Jaimini, as quoted by Mm. Gopinath Kaviraj in an article, improves this etymological meaning by adding a few very significant expressions. The derivative means of the term *mantra* that he gives is as follows — *mantrādi cinmarīcayaḥ tadvācakatvād vaikharī varṇavīlāsa-bhūtanāṁ vidyānām mananāt trāṇatā*. That is, *mantras*, etc, are of the nature of the effulgence of the consciousness-light (*cinmarīcayaḥ*), the word in gross form (i.e. ordinary words used by common man in his daily life) called *vaikarī varṇa* or *vāk* denotes the highest and purest spiritual knowledge embodying within them (i.e. *varna*) the consciousness-light, which, when grasped by men, saves them from the (trouble of) resorting to reflection by their intellect for understanding its real import. To put it in other words, the *mantras* heard or used by us in *vaikharī* or gross verbal form contain within their bosom the effulgence of the consciousness-light which shines forth when the potency 'lying dormant in it' is aroused, i.e. when the outer cover encasing the consciousness-light is broken open by the *guru* at the time of initiation (*dīkṣā*). The *mantras* received in this manner by the disciples and used during their spiritual practices provide them with the opportunity of obtaining a direct vision of the light of consciousness. When the *mantras* are used as an instrument for the revelation of consciousness (*caitanya*) contained therein, the disciple is not required to look for spiritual knowledge from any other external source. This is what the expression *trāṇatā* (saving) signifies when used by Śabara in his commentary.

Kinds of *mantra* and their use in *sādhanakriyā*

The word *mantra* is a generic term connoting different shades of meaning in different contexts. For example, *mantras* are used by people belonging to different levels for accomplishing different purposes. For instance, devout religious-minded persons utter *mantras* for propitiating their favourite deity in the course of their daily worship. These *mantras* are drawn from different sources, e.g. *Purānas*, *Stotras* (devotional texts), etc. It is impossible to conduct social rites, technically called *daśakarma* (ten kinds of rites), beginning with the ceremonial shaving of the head of a young child, the sacred thread ceremony, marriage, or offerings to the departed souls, etc, without using *mantras* as prescribed in the treatises on *Dharmaśāstra*. These *mantras*, borrowed freely from different texts, do not play however any role in the spiritual upliftment of the user. Such *mantras* are devoid of any 'potency', hence they are not relevant in the context of our present discussion.

Before we take up for discussion the nature of *mantra* and the role it plays in the spiritual discipline of a *sādhaka* following the Tantric mode of *sādhanā*, it would perhaps be useful if we give a bird's eye-view of the development of the concept of *mantra* from the Vedic tradition, and then turn our attention to the Tantric tradition.

When we study the Vedic literature to find out when the term *mantra* was first used, and what did the term connote there, we find that the term *mantra* was first used to denote the spontaneous utterances of the Vedic seers (*ṛṣis*) on their obtaining the vision of the spiritual Truth with the help of an 'inner eye' called *ārṣacakṣu*. The Vedic seers are traditional called *mantradraṣṭā*, the seers of *mantra* or the Spiritual Truth. They articulated their deep and sublime experiences spontaneously in their own words before their disciples. As ordinary words were incapable of conveying their vision of the Truth, very deep and complex, they had to employ symbolic language, pregnant with deep implications, which was later difficult to grasp by ordinary minds. Nonetheless, their words contained the vision of Truth in a condensed verbalised form, and the disciples of the Vedic seers had the privilege of listening to Vedic *mantras* coming directly from the lips of the seers of Truth, hence they could immediately grasp their 'inner' meaning. The Vedic *mantras* had a denotative power hidden in them, which got 'stirred up' as it were as the Vedic seers uttered them before their disciples. This led to revelation of the spiritual Truth seen by them as a result of their *saṅkalpa* (conscious resolve). Others who came later, in succession to the direct disciples, could not decipher the hidden meaning in the Vedic *mantras*, but, realising their sacredness because they had been uttered by seers, made great efforts to preserve their outward verbal structure and then pass them on orally to their disciples. Thus the process of oral transmission started. The Vedic *mantras*, embodying the esoteric experiences of Vedic seers, came down orally through a chain of disciples without any 'distortion', but their true meaning remained hidden. However, some seekers of spiritual truth succeeded to a great extent in decoding their hidden meaning by elevating themselves to that level of consciousness on which the supreme Truth was 'seen' by the seers. Sri Aurobindo and Srimat Anirvan are two such well-known examples in our times who developed extraordinary powers through their *sādhanā*, which enabled them to see intuitively their hidden meaning. They have conveyed their findings in the field in their writings.

Looking from the point of view of the verbal structure, the Vedic *mantras* are mostly multi-worded complete sentences, which are difficult for the spiritual practitioners to use for their spiritual elevation. The *Brāhmaṇa* texts however have found their utility in the performance of different kinds of sacrifices for obtaining mundane results. The focus of the *Brāhmaṇa* texts is to secure the welfare of the sacrificer on the mundane levels, but they are least concerned with the spiritual life of man.

However, a few *mantras* occurring in *Ṛgveda Saṁhitā* (II, 3, 12) and the *Atharvaveda Saṁhitā* (IX, 25, 27) surprisingly refer to a theory pertaining to the nature of *vāk* or speech, which has deep spiritual ramifications. They mention four levels of speech of *vāk* enshrined in the *mantra*, but does not spell out what these levels of speech are, neither whether these levels have any relevance in the spiritual field. Taking clue from these Vedic *mantras*, Bhartṛhari, the celebrated grammarian philosopher (ca. 5 cent. AD) formulated the philosophy of *vāk* (Primordial Word) in his famous work *Vākyapadīya*. According to him, the four levels of *vāk* in the descending order from subtlest to grossest are *parā*, *paśyantī*, *madhyamā* and *vaikharī*.

While the *vaikharī* represents *vāk* in grossest form, the form we use for communication in our daily life, the otherthree forms, *parā*, *paśyantī* and *madhyamā* are very subtle, therefore beyond the reach of our mind. They —*parā, paśyantī* and *madhyamā* — represent the *śakti* which is enshrined in the gross form of *vāk*, i.e. *vaikharī*. This *śakti* underlying *vaikharī vāk* is designated as the *vīrya* (potency) innate in the ordinary word. It may be mentioned in this context that some *yogins* are well known for possessing the extraordinary power to use the 'potency' lying encased within the word in *vaikharī* (gross) form to materialise the gross objects denoted by the particular word by 'concentrating' on it, thereafter unlocking the potency (*vīrya*) lying innate in it. There are several instances of amazing feats demonstrated by some Indian *yogins*, miracles which cannot otherwise be explained. This is true not only of Indian *yogins* but also of spiritual masters of other countries. For example, it is said in the Bible that the Lord said "Let there be Light" and there was light, illuminating and revealing everything. It might appear as a miracle to ignorant persons but it can be explained on the basis of the theory of *vāk* mentioned above.

Let us now turn our attention to the *mantra*, the role it plays in the spiritual life of a seeker of truth, and the manner it secures their spiritual elevation. It is well known that the spiritual master or *guru* 'implants' the *mantra* in the psychophysical apparatus of the disciple during initiation (*dīkṣā*), after it is purged of impurities. The Advaita Śaivites of Kashmir hold that with the influx of divine grace from the Supreme Lord through the *guru* into the spiritual seeker, the thick crust of basic defilement, the *āṇavamala* caused by the Supreme Lord assuming self-contraction, gets 'broken' when his initiation takes place and when the divine *mantra* is implanted in him. It is said that when the spiritual master 'gives' him the *mantra* for use in spiritual practices, like repetition of *mantra* (*japa*) during control of *prāṇavāyu* (technically called *prāṇāyāma*) or for meditation (*dhyāna*), etc, he first arouses the *śakti* or potency lying encased in the *mantra*, and thereby 'enlivens' the *mantra*, drawing the consciousness energy (*caitanya śakti*) from the *Parā-vāk*. The *guru* alone has access to that level of *vāk* from which he can 'draw' *śakti* and transform the *mantra* in gross *vaikharī* form into what has been called *caitanya mantra* — the *mantra* becoming 'alive' with the 'arousal' of *śakti* lying latent in it. This interpretation of *mantra śakti* is given by Tantric masters, which is in conformity with the Kriyā Yoga advocated by them.

It may be mentioned here that the Vedic tradition, prescribing the path of spiritual knowledge as a mode of spiritual discipline to be followed by spiritual practitioners, heldss similar views about the role of *mantra* in *sādhanā*. The *Yajurveda Saṁhitā* refers to the *haṁsa mantra* which was used by the spiritual practitioners in their *sādhanā*. The term *haṁsa* represents *so 'ham* ("That I am") arranged in reverse form, which was capable of bringing about self-realisation by the spiritual practitioners as *ahaṁ Brahmāsmi*, "I am *Brahman*". As a matter of fact, when the *Upaniṣads* speak about the *mahāvākyas* (the 'great sentences' conveying the spiritual experiences in different steps), this very idea about the role of *mantra* in *sādhanā* is implicit there.

The role of the *mahāvākyas* in the *sādhanā* as laid down in the *Upaniṣads* needs a little elaboration. It is said that as soon as the spiritual master or *guru* utters the *mantra* "*tattvamasī*" (you are that) before the disciple who has acquired all the qualities needed for following the path of knowledge, and who has also succeeded in cleansing fully his *antaḥkaraṇa* (internal sense faculty), he grasps the highest spiritual knowledge contained in this great *mantra* through reflection (*manana*), deep and continued reflection (*nididhyāsana*) in trance (*samādhi* of the *savikalpa* type). The Great Word contains within its verbal form the *śakti* (potency), which is manifested spontaneously the moment the *guru* utters it (the word). He immediately begins experiencing "I am *Brahman*" (*ahaṁ brahmāsmi*). This is called *anubhavavākya*, i.e. the expression conveying the highest spiritual experience. This expression conveying the spiritual experience of the *sādhaka* is, in fact, an echo of the *haṁsa mantra* (*so'ham*) mentioned in the Vedic *Saṁhitā* texts. As the *sādhaka* turns around to experience his surroundings, he discovers the presence of his consciousness nature (*caitanya*) everywhere (*sarvaṁ khalvidaṁ Brahma*). The entire surroundings are experienced by the *sādhaka* as having undergone a total change. His own being-experience expands from individual being-experience into universal being-experience, i.e. *Brahman*. He is filled with ecstatic delight. When he reaches the peak of his spiritual path, his individual being-experience melts, as it were, into the Universal, that is the indescribable state of spiritual realisation which the Advaita Śaivites of Kashmir call pure '*bodha*' (self-experience). The *sādhaka* then gets immersed in his fullness-nature (*akhaṇḍa svarūpa*).

As is clear from ths brief account of modes of spiritual discipline followed by the *sādhakas* belonging to the Tantric as well as to the Vedic tradition, the role of the *mantras* 'given' by the *guru* to their disciples plays a pivotal role in their spiritual elevation, culminating in the achievement of the ultimate Goal.

Let us now turn our attention to another aspect of the nature of *mantra*, namely the structural aspect. We have already mentioned that the Vedic *mantras* comprise complete sentences. It is obvious that the Vedic *mantras*, found in the multi-worded form embodying the Truth experiences of the Vedic seers, cannot be used by the *sādhakas* for their spiritual elevation. The *mantras* must be short so that they can be uttered with ease during contemplation or meditation. We find some short *mantras* comprised of a few words in later texts like the *Purānas* and devotional poems, etc, but these have also not been found useful by the *sādhakas* for the performance of *sādhanā*.

The Tantric *bījamantras*, on the other hand, have found favour with the practitioners of spiritual discipline. The *bījamantras* represent certain speech sounds, called *mātrika varṇas*, coalesced together and put in an 'encased form' (*sampuṭita*). Since the component of *bījamantras* are *mātrikā varṇas*, i.e. letters symbolising the spiritual energy or the consciousness force (*Śakti*), they (*bījamantras*) symbolise the consciousness energy encased within, which, when used properly during the practice of *sādhanā*, are capable of generating the experience of his real consciousness nature in the *sādhaka*. The *bījamantras* are likened to the 'seed' which, when implanted in the pure psychophysical framework of the *sādhaka* by the *guru*, fructifies in the course of his *sādhanā* and produces the desired result.

The origin of the *bījamantras* can be traced back to the Vedic times; the *praṇavamantra* is the classical example of the Vedic *bījamantra*. As is well known, the *Māṇḍukyopaniṣad* explains the significance of the *praṇavamantra* in philosophical terms. The Tantric texts mention a large number of *bījamantras*, which have been collected from different texts and listed in the *Mantrābhidhānakośa*, a dictionary of Tantric *mantras*, along with short explanations.

We do not know exactly how the *bījamantras* have come into existence. Is there any human author who created them? We however come across a reference in the first *āhnika* of the *Tantrāloka* by Abhinavagupta where the probable origin of *bījamantras* is given. It is said there that *bījamantras* originated from *sañjalpa*, i.e. sounds escaping involuntarily from the lips of a *yogin* during the transitional period from the state of trance (*samādhi*) to the normal state of consciousness or awareness. The yogin is then in a state of half-trance (*samādhi*) and half-waking condition, being in a spiritually-intoxicated state, and having no conscious control over his sense faculties. It is believed that during *samādhi* the *yogin* has wonderful spiritual experiences or visions, which he is unable to articulate, or wish to communicate. He only mutters something, which apparently does not appear to convey any meaning. These apparently meaningless sounds, condensed or juxtaposed one over the other, were heard by persons who were nearby, and constitute what is called *bījamantras*. These *mantras* contain a natural 'potency' or *śakti*, having been uttered by a *yogin*, and are therefore capable of revealing the power of consciousness power (*caitanya śakti*).

There is a corroborative evidence about this explanation provided by Abhinavagupta from the spiritual life of many *sādhakas*. The Pātañjala-Yoga also refers to *sañjalpa* (muttering of sounds) indicative of the deep spiritual experiences of *yogins* during the state of *samprajñāta samādhi*, but it does not talk about the origin of *bījamantras* for obvious reasons.

~CHAPTER IX~

Modes of Spiritual Discipline
(*Sādhanakriyā*)
in the Tāntrika Tradition

It is a well known fact that the highest spiritual wisdom has come down to us through two channels, technically called the *Nigama* and the *Āgama*. The *Nigama* represents the Vedic lore, comprising the *Saṁhitās* (collection of accounts of deep and sublime experiences of the spiritual Truth by the Vedic seers), the *Brāhmaṇas* (texts dealing with Vedic rituals), the *Āraṇyakas* and the *Upaniṣads* (containing dialogues on spiritual subjects between sages and their inquisitive disciples). The *Āgamas* embody spiritual wisdom revealed through dialogues between the Supreme Lord Śiva and her consort Devī or Pārvatī, the latter acting as the interlocutor or the other way round.

It is also well known that Indian philosophy in general is pragmatic in outlook inasmuch as it aims at securing the spiritual elevation of man and the betterment of the quality of his life. This is eloquently testified by the bold assertion made by Maitreyi before her husband Yājñavalkya thus: "What is the use of that (philosophical discussion in abstract terms) which cannot make me immortal" (*tenāhaṁ kiṁ kuryāṁ yenāham amṛtā na syām*). It is for this reason that the Indian spiritual thinkers have always tried to find out the means for attaining immortality (*amṛtattva*), the ultimate goal in life.

The different schools of Indian philosophical thought emanating from the Vedic lore prescribed the path of knowledge (*jñāna mārga*) as the mode of spiritual discipline for attaining the ultimate goal in life. But the *Āgamas* prescribe the performance of certain spiritual practices (*kriyā*) that spiritual seekers have to follow for attaining the supreme Goal.

The path of knowledge cannot be followed by one and all *sādhakas*, because it pre-supposes the acquisition of certain qualities pertaining to spiritual knowledge (*jñāna*), e.g. taking up the study of the Scriptures and reflecting on their purport, etc. This implies that the path of knowledge can be followed only by select *sādhakas* who possess the necessary qualifications, e.g. proficiency in the study of the Scriptures. In this context, it may be pointed out that, unlike the schools following the *Āgamas*, the different schools of Indian philosophical thought emanating from the Vedic lore prescribe only one particular mode of spiritual discipline for all *sādhakas*, over-looking their individual capacities and inclinations. The schools based on the *Āgamas* always take into consideration the capacity and inclination of the *sādhakas* while laying down the path of spiritual discipline for them. The spiritual practices laid down in the *Āgamas* vary, taking into consideration the capacity of the individual *sādhaka*. The mode of spiritual discipline (*sādhanā*) involving *kriyā*, as laid down in the *Āgamas*, does not require any kind of preparation on the part of the *sādhakas* unlike their counterpart who adopt the path of knowledge according to the Vedic tradition. The path of *kriyā* is open to all those who have received the divine grace through a *guru* and have undergone initiation (*dīkṣā*). Men and women belonging to all *varṇas*, all castes, can follow the path of *kriyā* after the influx of divine grace in them which makes them eligible for following this path of *sādhanā*. The descent of divine grace on the *sādhakas*, in the Tantric view, marks the turning point in their spiritual life; it opens the door to them to step into the realm of spirit. The Tantric texts point out that the *sādhakas* can make efforts on their own to purify their psycho-physical apparatus and can also thus make some progress in the spiritual path, but they cannot cross the barrier created by the Supreme Being by assuming voluntary self-limitation (*saṅkoca*), technically called *nigraha*, to become the multiplicity of subjects, objects of knowledge, etc. The obstacle in the form of self-limitation can be nullified only by *anugraha*, the opposite of *nigraha*, i.e. the influx of the divine grace which is flowing ceaselessly and naturally from the Supreme Lord but is available only to those who open themselves up to hold it.

Upāyas (modes of spiritual discipline)

The *Āgamas* prescribe a number of modes of spiritual discipline (*upāyas*) in accordance with the varying capacity and inclination of individual *sādhakas*. The choice of the particular mode of spiritual discipline that a particular *sādhaka* will have to adopt does not lie with him, but is determined by the intensity of the divine grace received by him. It is held in the Āgamic tradition that the more intense the divine grace received by a *sādhaka*, the lesser efforts he will have to put in to realise his ultimate goal. The Advaita Śaiva writers from Kashmir have discussed all these points threadbare in texts like the *Tantrāloka* and the *Tantrasāra*. It has been said there that the *guru* does not only give his disciple a glimpse of his real divine nature at the time of initiation, but he also indicates to him the path he has to follow to realise his true nature, keeping in view the intensity of the divine grace received by him as well as his inclination and his capability.

The Advaita Śaivites of Kashmir mention three major *upāyas* or modes of spiritual discipline based on the functioning of the divine Śakti in three different forms, namely, *icchā* (power as will), *jñāna* (power of knowledge) and *kriyā* (power of act). Incidentally, it may be mentioned here that this triad of the divine Śakti is held responsible for the Divine Being's self-manifestation as the world. Therefore it stands to reason that the same Śakti should singly play a crucial role in the spiritual life of *sādhakas* by restoring to them their divine nature.

Different *upāyas* or modes of spiritual discipline are prescribed by the Advaita Śaivites of Kashmir in the *Śāmbhavopāya*, the *Śāktopāya* and the *Āṇavapāya* for different categories of *sādhakas*. These *upāyas* are named *icchopāya* (*upāya* or mode of spiritual discipline in which *icchāśakti* plays a dominant role), *jñānopāya* (*upāya* in which *jñānaśakti* plays a dominant role) and *kriyopāya* in which *kriyāśakti* plays a dominant role).

Since most of the Śākta Tantras stress on the performance of various kinds of *kriyā* (spiritual practices) in their mode of spiritual discipline, they give an elaborate description of various kinds of spiritual practices to be followed by *sādhakas*. Some spiritual practices relate to making the physical body a fit instrument for the performance of *sādhanā*, e.g. *Haṭhayoga*, others relate to spiritual practices for the purification of the psycho-physical apparatus, etc. The Advaita Śaivites of Kashmir, drawing their inspiration from the *Bhairava Tantras*, formulate their mode of *sādhanā* based on *kriyā*. They recognise that most *sādhakas* are unable to follow the path of spiritual discipline laid down under *śāmbhava* or *śākta upāya* on account of the mildness of divine grace received by them, therefore they are forced to adopt *āṇavopāya* or the *kriyopāya*, in which certain spiritual practices play the dominant role.

Among the various kinds of spiritual practices of prescribed in the *Āgamas* for the *sādhakas* following *kriyopāya* are *bhāvanā* (imaginative meditation), *japa* (repetition of the sacred *mantra* given by the *guru*) and *prāṇoccāra* (the use of *prāṇaśakti,* 'vital power', for securing spiritual upliftment), culminating in the realisation of their real divine nature.

The *Vijñāna Bhairava Tantra* enumerates 112 methods of *dhāraṇās* (modes of concentration) for achieving union with the divine. It describes the spiritual instructions on *dhāraṇās* as *nistaraṅga upadeśa*, i.e. instructions for achieving the 'waveless' state of mind when it becomes totally free from thought-constructs (*vikalpa*). Mind is said to possess a natural propensity to undergo modifications in accordance with the object of knowledge reflected in it, or the tendency to imagine concepts or ideas without any break. The *Vijñāna Bhairava* therefore prescribes methods for 'emptying' the mind totally, thereby achieving a state of freedom from thought-constructs (*nirvikalpa*). It is only then that the *sādhaka* is able to discover his true nature reflected in a fully 'empty' mind, namely a self-effulgent or self-shining pure consciousness (*caitanya*). It may be mentioned here that this description of *dhāraṇā* is very much similar to that of *cittavṛttinirodha*, i.e. the perfect cessation of all modifications of *citta* mentioned in the *Yogasūtra* of Patañjali.

It has been stated in the *Vijñāna Bhairava* that, though the number of *dhāraṇās* prescribed there is 112, a *sādhaka* need not perform all of them as each of them singly is capable of leading to the achievement of the supreme Goal, i.e. attainment of the form of Lord Bhairava.

The mode of spiritual discipline involving the use of *prāṇaśakti* for securing spiritual upliftment, technically called *praṇoccāra*, is universally accepted by all schools emanating from the *Āgamas* as the best mode of spiritual practice. It is also called *Kuṇḍalinī Yoga*. Before we describe briefly this mode of spiritual discipline it would perhaps be useful to know the nature of *prāṇa*, the various manifestations of *prāṇaśakti*, and the role it plays in the *sādhanā* included under *āṇavopaya* by the Advaita Śaivites.

It may be mentioned in this connection that though the mode of *sādhanā* involving the use of *prāṇaśakti* does not find place in the Vedic spiritual tradition, light on the nature of *prāna* has been shed in some ancient *Upaniṣads*, which we propose to mention briefly in this context. It plays a major role in the life of those spiritual seekers who follow the paths laid down in the *Āgamas*.

Nature of *prāṇa* and its role in *sādhanā* (*prāṇoccāra*)

All living beings existing in this world in embodied condition are conscious of the functioning of *prāṇa* (vital breath) in their physical body to keep them alive and active. But, generally speaking, they are ignorant about its genesis, nature and the role in plays in their mundane life. Some schools of Indian philosophical thought were more inclined towards the application of their philosophical thoughts to man's life in the world in view of its qualitative improvement rather than merely formulating grand metaphysical theories divorced from life, their stress being on laying down the path of spiritual discipline involving *prāṇa*. The concept of *prāṇa* constitutes an integral part of these schools. All these schools of Indian philosophical thought, as well as some yoga practitioners not belonging to any particular traditional thought-current, throw light on this concept of *prāṇa*, the nature of which is shrouded in mystery. These schools explore the possibility of employing *prāṇaśakti* (vital force) for the spiritual elevation of the spiritual seekers, incorporating it in their mode of spiritual discipline (*sādhanā*).

Treatment of *prāṇa* in some select ancient Upaniṣads

It is a well known fact that the *Upaniṣads* constitute the earliest storehouse of rich spiritual wisdom. Let us therefore begin our inquiry into the nature of *prāṇa* in a historical perspective as delineated in some select *Upaniṣads*. *Prāṇa* originally signified breath, as breath appeared to constitute the life in living embodied beings; it later came to denote the life principle. Just as *prāṇa* came to be depicted as the life-principle in man, the life-principle in the universe came also to be designated as *praṇa*. "Just as all the spokes of a wheel are centred in its navel, similarly all these beings, in fact, everything that exists in the universe, is centred in *prāṇa*", Sanatkumāra tells Nārada in the *Taittirīya Upaniṣad* (viii, 5, 1). The same *Upaniṣad* tells us that when Uṣasti Cākrāyāṇa was asked what might be substratum of all things in the world, he replied that it was *prāṇa*, for "verily it is *prāṇa* that all things enter, and it is from *prāṇa* they original sprang". Raivataka sees a correspondence between the microcosm and the macrocosm when he says that just as air (*vāyu*) is the life-principle of the universe, breath (*prāṇavāyu*) is the life-principle in man. *Prāṇa* is the final absorbent; when a man sleeps, his speech is reduced to *prāṇa*, his eyes, ears and minds, all are absorbed in *prāṇa*.

The *Kauṣītakī Upaniṣad* holds *prāṇa* to be identical with the ultimate Reality, the *Brahman*. At another place, this *Upaniṣad* identifies *prāṇa* with life.

The *Taittirīya Upaniṣad* depicts *prāṇa* as of the nature of a metaphysical principle (*tattva*) existing independently and outside the physical body of the embodied beings. It conceives *prāṇa* as identical with the *Brahman*, the all-pervading Reality or *Caitanya,* telling us that the spiritual seekers have 'known' it (from their spiritual experience) to be the all-pervading Reality. They have 'seen' all beings emanating from *prāṇa*; having emerged from *prāṇa*, they are sustained by *prāṇa*, and at the end, that is at the time of cosmic dissolution, they merge in *prāṇa* (Taitt. Up. III, 3).

At another place, the same *Upaniṣad* equates *prāṇa*, the core principle, with the *ātman* (self) residing in the physical bodies of individual beings. Here, *prāṇa* is spoken of not as the all-pervading Reality, the substratum of world manifestation, but as the core principle permeating the physical bodies of all embodied beings. It is said here that as *prāṇa* enters in the physical bodies of all embodied beings, they become alive. All gods, men and subhuman creatures are enlivened by the presence of *prāṇa* in their physical frame. The duration of the existence of *prāṇa* in their physical bodies determines the span of their life (*āyu*); therefore *prāṇa* can be equated with life.

The *Praśnopaniṣad*, while generally endorsing these views expressed in the *Taittirīya Upaniṣad* about the oneness of the self, the core being with the *prāṇa*, holds that they are one in essence only. The self (*ātman*) is the cause of *prāṇa*; their mutual relation is one of cause and effect. Having been produced from the Self (meaning in this context the universal self), when *prāṇa* 'enters' the physical body of an embodied being along with the self (*ātman*), *prana* 'follows closely' 'the self like a shadow' following the physical body (of man) in broad daylight.

Elsewhere, we find in the same *Upaniṣad* that *prāṇa* is conceived as the *śakti* of *caitanya*, which is held to be ceaselessly operating while fused with *caitanya*. This is obvious from the statement occurring in this *Upaniṣad* describing *prāṇa* to be of the nature of 'fire' (*agni*), always remaining 'awake' (i.e. ablaze) in the physical bodies of all embodied beings.

By conceptualising the *prāṇa śakti* as 'fire', this *Upaniṣad* seems to suggest that the 'prāṇic fire' (the vital force in the form of spiritual fire) existing within the physical body must be propitiated by every individual being, nourished and kept 'ablaze' by offering daily oblations in it. This is necessary on the part of the individual being for prolonging his life.

Identifying the *prāṇa śakti*'s ceaselessly functioning in the physical framework of every embodied being with *prāṇa vāyu* (vital breath), the *Paraśnopaniṣad* describes the manner it (*prāṇavāyu*) functions in five forms in every embodied being. Using a metaphor, sage Pippalāda tells Āśvalāyana that just as an emperor directs his subordinate officers to go to different parts in his kingdom and take their seats there, and thereafter also assigns to them different duties to perform, in the same way *prāṇa śakti*, the lord of *prāṇa vāyu*, places them in the different parts of the body and assists them individually with different tasks to carry on.

For example, *prāṇaśakti* assigns a seat to *apāna vāyu* in the region of *pāyu* and *upastha* (the generative and excretory organ), and to *prāṇavāyu* in the region of the mouth and nostrils. *Prāṇaśakti* puts the *samānavāyu* in the midpart, i.e. the navel (*nābhi*) region which carries on the task of digestion and assimilation of food, resulting in the production of 'fire' or a physical energy having seven-tongued 'flames of physical power'. *Prāṇaśakti* assigns a place to *vyāna vāyu* in the region of the heart wherefrom it spreads to all parts of the body, flowing through the network of thousands of *nāḍīs* (channels), making it sentient; it assigns *udānavāyu* a place at the bottom part from where it moves up through the channel called *suṣumṇā*, taking the virtuous ones up through the crown in the head to their heavenly abode, and the sinful to the mundane level to suffer the consequences of their actions.

Nature of *prāṇa* in some schools of Indian Philosophy

Let us now turn our attention to the various schools of Indian philosophy which speak about *prāṇa*'s metaphysical category. Taking a clue from the ancient *Upaniṣads* like the *Chāndogya Upaniṣad*, *Taittirīya Upaniṣad*, *Bṛhadāraṇyaka Upaniṣad* (I, 58), the Advaita

Vedāntins of Śaṅkara's School take *prāṇa* to signify the *prāṇavāyu* (vital breath) only, which is included in the list of metaphysical categories postulated by them. It is a part and parcel of the world creation in its macrocosmic form and of embodied individuals in the microcosmic form. *Prāṇavāyu* is said to be fivefold, namely *prāṇa*, *apāna*, *udāna*, *vyāna* and *samāna*, product of the *rājasic* element of *Māyā śakti*. It is held to be associated with the subtle body (*sūkṣma śarīra*) of every embodied individual. Since the subtle body (*sukṣma śarīra*) of an embodied being is held to be relatively permanent compared to the gross body (*sthūla śarīra*), having come into existence at the time of the first creation of the world, the five-fold *prāṇa vāyus* are held to be permanent as they do not cease to exist in him with the cessation of the gross body at the time of death. It is said to migrate to another physical body together with its locus, the subtle body, when the embodied being is born.

The five-fold *prāṇa vāyu* functions ceaselessly located in different parts of the physical body of individual beings, controlling and regulating the activity of various physiological organs.

Since the five-fold *prāṇa vāyu* is said to be the product of *Māyā śakti*, it is said to constitute the *prāṇamaya kośa*, one of the sheaths that veils the real nature of the self (*ātman*). This is because *Mayā śakti* operating on the mundane level is said to manifest the phenomenal world by operating her powers of concealment and projection (*āvaraṇa vikṣepa*). The *prāṇamaya kośa*, being a product of *Māyā śakti* and existing as a constituent element of the subtle body, discharges that task of concealment of the self.

The *Yoga Sūtra* of Patañjali also refers to *prāṇa* or *prāṇavāyu* (vital breath) in the context of the spiritual discipline described in the *Sādhanapāda*. The nature of *prāṇavāyu* as such has not been discussed, but the necessity of practising *prāṇāyāma* (control of outgoing and incoming breaths) has been discussed in *sūtra* II, 49. The control of breaths by regulating them, technically called *prāṇāyāma*, leads to the rise of *apāna vāyu* through the middle channel up to the crown of the head, resulting in stillness of *citta* (internal organ of knowledge) on the one hand, and its cleansing on the other. Normally the *citta* is covered by a thick veil of residual impressions of past actions, which prevents the mirror-like *citta* dominated by the *sattva guṇa* to shine. The practice of *prāṇāyāma* for a long time results in the removal of this thick veil, culminating in the removal of defilements from *citta* and the reflection of the light of consciousness in its perfect mirror-like form. According to the Patañjala Yoga, the spiritual aspirant can thus reach the ultimate goal with the help of *prāṇavayu* (vital breath).

Out of the six orthodox schools of Indian philosophy, only two schools, namely the Advaita Vedānta of Śaṅkara and the Pātañjala Yoga School speak about *prāṇaśakti*, shedding light on its relevance and place in their mode of spiritual discipline.

We may conclude this discussion about the nature and function of *prāṇa śakti* with a quotation from "A Constructive Survey of the Philosophy of Upaniṣads" by R.D. Ranade (Poona 1929, p. 92): "*Prāṇa* is life from the biological point of view, consciousness (*caitanya*) from the psychological point of view and the *ātman* (self) from the metaphysical point of view".

Nature of *prāṇa* and its place in *sādhanakriyā* in the Āgamic tradition

Let us now turn our attention to the views of the Advaita Śaiva School of Kashmir, based on the *Āgamas*, on the nature of *prāṇaśakti* (vital force) and its gross manifestation, *prāṇavāyu* (vital breath), operating in the physical bodies of all living beings and keeping them alive and sentient (*cetanavat*). The Advaita Śaivites hold that *prāṇaśakti* and *Saṁvid* or *caitanya* (pure consciousness), forming the core of being of all embodied individuals, are so closely knit together that the former can be adopted by spiritual seekers as the instrument for reaching *Saṁvid*, the self. It is for this reason that they give a prominent place to both *prāṇaśakti* (vital force) and *prāṇa vāyu* (vital breath) in their scheme of spiritual discipline (*sādhanā*).

Bhaṭṭa Kallaṭa, disciple of sage Vasugupta the founder of the Advaita Śaiva School in Kashmir, and himself founder of the Spanda branch of Śaiva thought, has shed light on the origin of *prāṇaśakti* (vital force) in his scheme of creation. His statement in some unspecified text has been quoted by both Abhinavagupta and his disciple Kṣemarāja to state the Advaita Śaiva position on this subject. It is said there that *Saṁvid* (Supreme Consciousness) assumes the form of *prāṇaśakti* at the beginning of the creation of the world. The *praṇaśakti* referred to is obviously the cosmic *prāṇaśakti*, not the individual *prāṇaśakti* seen by us functioning in the physical bodies of all embodied beings.

Kallaṭa, however, has not spelled out how *Saṁvid* assumes the form of *prāṇaśakti*. Abhinavagupta in his *Tantrāloka* has described the manner in which *Saṁvid* (supreme consciousness), or precisely speaking *Saṁvid Devī* (consciousness *śakti*), pulsating ceaselessly coalesced with *Saṁvid*, takes the form of *prāṇaśakti* in course of Her (*Saṁvid Devī*'s) involution or descent as the universe. *Saṁvid*, according to him, shines as the undifferentiated Illumination (*akhaṇḍa prakāśa*) on the highest level of existence prior to the manifestation of the world. *Saṁvid* then has the self-reflective experience (*parāmarśa*) of His fullness-nature (*pūrṇatva*) in the form of *pūrṇāhaṁtā* (integral I-experience). There is then no trace of the universe in His self-experience (*parāmarśa*), not even a faint idea of the universe to be manifested as the object of experience of that level of involution, namely *Śivatattva*. *Saṁvid* then is said to remain immersed in His fullness-nature, experiencing massive bliss in condensed form (*ghanībhūta ānanda*), as it were.

In order to manifest Himself as the universe out of His free will (*svecchayā*), exercising His power of divine Freedom (*svātantraya śakti*), *Saṁvid* is first said to eclipse His transcendent nature (*anuttararūpa*) by assuming voluntarily a contraction (*saṅkoca* or *nigraha*) which is reflected in the form of change in His self-experience (*parāmarśa*). He then has no longer the self-experience as *pūrṇāham* (integral experience, signifying His fullness nature). A void (*śūnya*) is created in His self-experience as it were, which has been technically described as *nabha* or *ākāśa* (lit. sky). *Saṁvid*'s self-experience as 'I' (*aham*) however does not disappear fully on the level of *Śaktitattva*, existing just below the *Śivatattva*, but persists in a somewhat 'unclear form' (*dhyāmala*) due to the self-imposed contraction and the creation of void (*śūnya*) on that level. Abhinavagupta justifies the creation of void (*śūnya*) in His self-experience on the level of *Śaktitattva*, adducing a logical reasoning. According to him, the creation of void in the subject's self-experience is an essential precondition for the appearance of the object symbolized by the 'this-ness' (*idam*) to His self-experience.

Another reason that can be given for explaining the creation of void (*śūnya*) in His self-experience may be stated this way. After *Saṁvid*'s self-experience as 'I' (*aham*) gets somewhat hazy and clouded, following the voluntary assumption of contraction, its counterpart, the experience of 'this-ness' (*idam*) not having appeared by then, i.e. on the level of *Śaktitattva* in His self-experience, the creation of vacuum then is nothing but a logical necessity.

Jayaratha, the commentator, in his *vivṛti* on the *Tantrāloka* of Abhinavagupta states that the self-contracted subject (*aham*) or the experiencer associated with the void (*śūṇya*) as the object of experience on the level of *Śaktitattva* can be called the *śūnya pramātā* (the experiencer of the Void). He has cited the experience of a *yogin* in the state of *asamprajñāta samādhi* (objectless trance) mentioned in the Pātañjala Yoga philosophy as a parallel to the self-experience by a *śūnya pramātā* (experiencer of the void) when he experiences total vacuity, represented in verbal form by "*neti*, *neti*" (not this, not this). The commentator takes great pains in interpreting the significance of the double negative to describe this experience of the *yogin*. According to him, the first expression of *neti* (not this) to convey the experience of vacuity denotes the non-existence of the *yogin*'s being (*sattā*), and the second expression of *neti* the non-existence of non-existence.

It is held by the Advaita Śaivites that as *Saṁvid* undergoes further involution from the level of *Śaktitattva* to the level of *Sadāśiva tattva*, a schism appears spontaneously, as it were, in his self-experience (*parāmarśa*), as a result of which two poles of experience are created as it were, that of the pure or universal experiencer and the pure or universal object, symbolised by *aham* and *idam* respectively. The self-experience of *Saṁvid* as *Aham* shines clearly in the mirror of consciousness, which serves as the locus or substratum of all His self-experience on the level of *Sadāśiva tattva*, while His self-experience as *idam* (this-ness) remains faint or indistinct on account of its just 'popping up', as it were, in His self-experience. It may be mentioned here that both kinds of self-experiences, as the pure subject (*aham*) and the pure Object (*idam*), remain universal (*viśvātamaka*) in form and in-separately fused in nature in the absence of the notion of duality (*dvaita*), this being totally absent on all the levels of existence in the sphere of pure creation (*śuddha adhva*).

When this happens, there is simultaneously an upsurge or flush of the divine Śakti, named *Saṁvid Devī* by Abhinavagupta, which till then had remained somewhat unruffled and welled up, as it were, within the bosom of *Saṁvid*. The pent up divine Śakti spills and begins flowing out from *Saṁvid* as a consequence of the flush of Śakti to 'unroll' (*unmeṣa*) the universe, first in 'ideal' form, i.e. as self-experience within *Saṁvid* experiencer, later taking concrete form in the spheres of *Māyā* and *Prakṛti*.

Simultaneously with the flowing out of the divine Śakti, the spillage (*ucchalana*) of Śakti occurs from the bosom of *Saṁvid*, which is manifested as *prāṇaśakti* (vital force). *Prāṇaśakti* is born in this way from the spillage of *Saṁvid Devī* or divine Śakti from the heart of *Saṁvid* in the sphere of pure creation or *Mahāmāyā*; probably this occurs on the level of *Īśvaratattva* (just below the level of *Sadāśiva-tattva*), though no text has mentioned explicitly the exact stage on which spillage of the divine Śakti from *Saṁvid* takes place.

If appears that when Kallaṭa speaks about the manifestation of *prāṇaśakti* out of *Saṁvid Devī* or the divine Śakti, he has the above mentioned process of involution of Śakti as the universe in mind. It was probably Abhinavagupta who for the first time explained when and how the *prāṇa śakti* actually makes its first appearance during the process of world-manifestation outlined in the above paragraphs.

Sometimes, the pulsations of the divine Śakti technically called *spanda* have been described in terms of a perennial series of contraction *(ṣaṅkoca)* and expansion (*prasāra*) of Śakti. The pulsation of *prāṇaśakti* is also sometimes depicted as waves of *śakti* in the form of *prāṇa*, rising and falling in the ocean of *Saṁvid* without bringing about any substantial change. Therefore, the pulsation of *prāṇaśakti* is given the name *Saṁvidormi* (wave in the ocean of *Saṁvid*).

It has been mentioned that *prāṇaśakti*, which first appears in creation in the course of the involution of divine Śakti (*Pārameśvarī Śakti*), is manifested in universal form, remaining inseparably fused with the *Parāsaṁvid* (Supreme Consciousness), and it is later, when *prāṇaśakti* takes its seat in the gross physical bodies of embodied beings in the sphere of *Māyā* and *Prakṛti*, that it assumes a limited form, appearing different from *Saṁvid*. Its functioning then is perceived within the physical bodies of all embodied beings, making them sentient and living.

Kṣemarāja, in his *Pratyabhijñā Hṛdayam* (*sūtra* 17) explains almost on the same lines the manifestation of *prāṇaśakti* in course of the involution of *Saṁvid* as the universe. Endorsing the Advaita Śaiva view that the manifestation of the universe represents the expansion (*vikāsa*) of *Saṁvid* in the form of the divine Śakti or *Saṁvid Devī*, pulsating ceaselessly coalesced with the *Parāsaṁvid* (Supreme Consciousness Being) or Śiva, Kṣemarāja tells us that the divine Śakti assumes the form of *prānaśakti* after 'concealing' her consciousness-nature (*cit śakti*) and then appears in the sphere of *māyā* (*aśuddha adhva*), taking its seat in the gross physical bodies of embodied beings, or in their intellect (*buddhi*) or some other constituent of their physical body. In this way, the *prāṇaśakti* associated with each and every gross physical body of all embodied beings becomes manifold under the influence of *māyā*.

The Advaita Śaivites hold that *prāṇaśakti* is the locus (*ādhāra*) for the creation of time (*kāla*) and space (*deśa*), which have not been given separate status as categories in their scheme of metaphysics, unlike in the Nyāya-Vaiśeṣika schools. It has been said in the *Tantrāloka* (Ah. VI, V.23) that as the divine Śakti in the form of *prāṇa* moves up and down from the point called *mulādhāra* to the crown of the head in the physical body, taking 60 units of time in twenty-four hours. Its path of movement up and down conforms the total number of movements of *prāṇa* known as *prāṇoccāra*, which according to the *Svacchanda Tantra* is 216000 in the lifetime of an embodied living being, after which it goes out of the physical body to merge with the universal *prāṇa*. Abhinavagupta, both in the *Tantrāloka* (Ah. VI) and the *Tantrasāra*, provided us with other details about the creation of time and space from the movement of *prāṇa*. All this he has done to show that the spiritual aspirants cannot succeed in transcending the barriers of time and space without employing *prāṇa* as a means to go beyond time and space to realise their Śiva-nature. The Advaita Śaivites have therefore given due importance to *praṇa* in their mode of spiritual discipline under the *āṇavopāya* prescribed for the least qualified or inferior kind of *sādhakas*.

Kṣemarāja, in *sūtra* 17 of the *Pratyabhijña Hṛdayam*, also refers to the *madhyanāḍī* (middle channel), existing in the gross physical bodies of all embodied beings, going upward from the *mūlādhāra*, i.e. the spinal centre located below the genitals, to the crown in the head, technically called *brahmarandhra* or the *sahasrāra* (the thousand-petalled lotus). He also mentions two other channels, *īḍā* and *piṅgalā*, running parallel to the middle one on the left and the right sides respectively along the spinal column. The two channels *iḍā* and *piṅgalā*, somewhat curved at the tips, join the middle channel *suṣumṇā* at the *ājñācakra* situated in the physical body between the two eyebrows. The *ājñācakra* is therefore described as the *triveṇī*, the confluence of three channels. Kṣemaraja also refers to the network of one thousand *nāḍīs* or channels spread all over the gross physical body, emerging from the two *nāḍīs* through which the *prāṇic* energy (*prāṇaśakti*) is said to flow to different limbs in the body.

Kṣemarāja has compared the emergence of the network of *nāḍīs* or channels coming from the middle one to the mid rib in a *palāśa* tree (*biutea frondosa*), in which veinlets are seen to emerge from the mid rib. It is said that as the consciousness power flows out in the form of *prāṇic* energy (*prāṇaśakti*) to different parts in the gross physical body constituted by insentient material elements, they become sentient-like and begin responding to external stimuli. The gross physical body becomes alive and active on account of all this.

It would perhaps not be out of place in this context to mention briefly the existence of six *cakras* existing at different points in the middle channel (*madhyanāḍī*), as well as their function. The existence of these *cakras* has been mentioned both by Abhinavagupta and Kṣemarāja, but the detailed account of their nature and function are seen in some later Śākta Upaniṣads and Tantric texts (like the *Gandharva Tantra*) and texts on Haṭhayoga (e.g. *Gheraṇda Saṁhitā*, *Ṣaṭcakranirupaṇa*, *Haṭha Yoga Pradīpikā*, etc), which are acceptable to the Advaita Śaiva *ācāryas*. The six *cakras*, enumerated from the bottom of the gross physical body, are *mulādhāracakra* located in the spinal column below the region of the genitals, *svādhiṣṭhānacakra* located in the spinal column above the region of the genitals, *maṇipūracakra,* existing in the region of the navel (*nābhi*), *anāhata cakra* located in the spinal column in the region of the heart, *viśuddha cakra* situated in the spinal column at the base of the throat, and *ājñācakra* located in the region between the two eyebrows in the gross body.

These *cakras* are named this way on account of their wheel-like appearance, and they provide a resting place for Śakti while rising up. The primary function of these *cakras* is to absorb *prāṇaśakti* from its macrocosmic form existing outside the body, mix it up with that which is existing within, and then distribute the amalgam of internal and external *prāṇaśakti* made on different *cakras* in the course of its movement both upward and downward in the middle channel. The *prāṇaśakti* gains more power as a consequence of mixing up the external *prāṇaśakti* with the internal one. When a spiritual aspirant is able to activate these centres or *cakras* by performing certain spiritual practices, filling them with *prāṇaśakti* in 'condensed form', he obtains different kinds of deep spiritual and occult experiences, indicating the extent of his spiritual elevation.

Though *prāṇaśakti* is held by the Advaita Śaivites to operate ceaselessly in the gross physical body (*sthūla deha*) of all embodied beings, it is not generally perceptible from outside. Two reasons can be given for this: *prāṇaśakti* is essentially of the nature of consciousness-force (*citśakti*), and it is too subtle to be grasped by the senses. Kṣemarāja gives an additional reason for this fact. According to him, *praṇaśakti* is the source of energy to all sense organs (*jñānendriyas*), which filled up with that power move out to seize the objects of knowledge. The senses, being the instrument for grasping external objects, cannot grasp the source of their energy, i.e. *prāṇaśakti*.

But when *prāṇaśakti* assumes a gross form in the course of further involution, it manifests itself as *prāṇavāyu* (vital breath) to sustain the physical body in embodied beings, it becomes palpable and is perceived as such by us all. It is well known that one of the infallible signs of life in embodied beings is the movement of *prāṇavāyu* in the form of inhalation and exhalation going on ceaselessly from birth to death. The *Svacchanda Tantra* tells us that a living being breathes in and out (*prāṇoccāra*) 216000 times in twenty-four hours.

The vital breath (*prāṇa vāyu*) is five-fold in accordance with its functioning at different locations in the gross physical body, and regulating the activities of different physiological organs in the body. These are the *prāṇa vāyu*, the *apāna vāyu*, the *samāna vayu*, the *udāna vāyu* and the *vyāna vāyu*.

The *Svacchanda Tantra* (IV, 235) describes *prāṇa* primarily as of the nature of the pulsation of Śakti (*spanda*), which arises spontaneous in the region *kanda* located below the genitive organ in the physical body. It moves upward naturally from the place of its origin to the core of the heart without being perceived by the embodied being. Simultaneously with this upward movement of *prāṇa*, an unstruck sound (*anāhata dhvani*) in the form of murmor arises, which remains inaudible to the embodied beings on account of its very low pitch. The movement of *prāṇa* in this manner (*prāṇoccāra*) is of little use to the spiritual aspirants, and is therefore ignored by them insofar as the performance of their spiritual discipline (*sādhanā*) is concerned. The movement of *prāṇa* and *apāna* then is seen in the form of continuous inhalation and exhalation of breath.

When, according to the Advaita Śaiva *ācāryas*, a spiritual aspirant, following the path of spiritual discipline called the *āṇavopāya*, makes conscious and deliberate efforts to make *prāṇa* in his physical body to move upward from the centre of his heart through the channel *iḍā* up to the spot called *dvadaśānta* situated at the distance of 12 fingers from the middle of eyebrows to above the crown of the head and then, getting it rested there for a while, thereafter make it move downward through the channel called *piṅgalā* back to the centre of his heart, then it called *apāna*. The spiritual aspirant as a consequence of this obtains deep spiritual experiences.

The mode of spiritual discipline briefly described in the above paragraph, called *prāṇoccāra* by the Advaita Śaiva *ācāryas*, is not very different from what is popularly known as *Kuṇḍalinī Yoga*. It may be pointed out here that *Kuṇḍalinī Yoga* as such does not find a place in the Vedic tradition, but it occupies a prominent place in Śākta and Śaiva traditions in which *kriyā* plays a dominant role in *sadhanā*. Mahamahopadhyaya Gopinath Kaviraj expressed this view in one of his essays on Kuṇḍalinī Yoga entitled *Kuṇḍalinī Rahasya* (the secret of Kundalini Yoga). Indeed it is for this reason that the orthodox schools of Indian philosophy emanating from the Vedic lore do not assign any role to *praṇaśakti* in their scheme of spiritual discipline (*sādhanā*). Also because these schools, to achieve the ultimate goal, prefer to follow the path of knowledge (*jñāna*) in their mode of spiritual discipline as against the path of *kriyā* adopted by the schools based on Tantra.

As has already been mentioned in the foregoing paragraphs, the Advaita Śaiva writers advise spiritual aspirants to follow the mode of *prāṇāyāma* (breath control) to secure the movement of *prāṇa* and *apāṇa* within their physical bodies. According to them, the spiritual aspirant must first, through the practice of *prāṇāyāma*, try to equalise the two breaths, *prāṇa* and *apāṇa vāyu*, which in the form of *śakti* are also called *ravi* (lit. sun) and *śaśi* (moon) respectively (T.A. IV. v.91). When the aspirant succeeds in his effort, the *udāna* lying asleep or dormant on the level of the *mulādhāra cakra* blazes forth, taking the form of *vahni* (fire), and it moves up through the *madhyadhāma* (middle channel) also known as *suṣumṇā nāḍī*, to reach the highest point on the crown of the head. This paves the way to the ascent of the consciousness energy normally lying coiled up in 3.5 folds (*balayas*) on the level of *mulādhara*. This coiled-up consciousness *śakti* is technically called *kuṇḍalinī śakti* or, precisely speaking, *adhaḥ kuṇḍalinī*.

Kuṇḍalini śakti gradually rises up following the path of *udāna vāyu* through the middle channel, till she reaches *lambikā* situated in the region of the palate, the crossroad of four *prāṇic* channels (*nāḍīs*) going in different directions in the physical body. She continues her upward journey to pierce the *brahmarandhra*, a canopy-like cover on the level of the crown, to reach and rest on the *dvadaśānta*. The *kuṇḍalinī śakti* resting there is called *ūrdha kuṇḍalinī*. The *udāna vāyu* then pervades the entire physical framework and is given the name *vyāna*, the all-pervading *vāyu*.

On consciousness-*śakti* achieving this state of highest elevation, the spiritual aspirant experiences an ecstatic delight, and his physical body gets drenched with spiritual ambrosia dripping from the *sahasrāra*. The task of *kuṇḍalinī śakti* does not end with this achievement. The *śakti* moves up and down in alternate sequence, once the blockages from the *madhyanāḍī* are removed by the ascent of *śakti* achieved by the spiritual aspirant, resulting in the destruction of defilements — *māyīya* and *kārma malas* together with their underlying residual impressions (*saṁskāras*) — making the physical body a perfect vehicle for achieving the ultimate goal in life, viz Śiva-nature.

As the consciousness-*śakti* passes through different wheel-like stations in her path of ascent to reach the Summit, the spiritual aspirants are said to have different kinds of spiritual experiences, such as hearing *anāhata nāda* (primordial sound) in different forms, or visualising the effulgence of consciousness in different degrees of brightness. All these supernormal spiritual experiences assure the spiritual seeker that he is on the right path, as they provide him with encouragement in pursuing their *sādhana* relentlessly till the goal is reached. The *Upaniṣads* echoes this with the advice — Arise, awake, stop not till the Goal is reached.

Quoting the *Gandharva Tantra*, the Advaita Śaiva texts describe the ten forms in which the primordial sound is experienced by the aspirant as he progresses to achieve the Goal: (1) *cin* sound, (2) *cincin* sound (3) sound made by *cīrāvaka* (cricket), (4) sound produced by a conch shell, (5) sound produced by a string instrument, (6) sound produced by a flute, (7) sound produced by a bell, (8) sound resembling thunder (9) sound produced by *rava* (humming of bees), (10) sound produced by a percussion instrument. When the aspirant is able to hear the *anāhata sound*, it indicates that the ultimate goal is not far away.

In the same way the *Āgamas* describe the gradation in the experience of the consciousness-illumination in different forms. The illumination can be dim and soothing in form, it may be dazzling like the sun and the moon. These spiritual experiences provide encouragement to the *sādhakas* in the pursuit of their ultimate Goal, i.e. their Śiva-nature.

~Chapter X~

The Supreme Goal, Śivatva

The Supreme Goal, according to the Śaiva Tantras, is the attainment of one's Divine Nature, *Śivatva*. It has already been observed that the Supreme Lord, in exercise of His divine Freedom, manifests Himself as the universe, in which He assumes different roles by contracting and concealing His divine Nature. It therefore stands to reason that He should by exercising His divine Freedom in the form of divine Grace to restore Himself to His original divine status which in fact should be the ultimate Destiny. It has therefore been rightly said that the Supreme Lord, during the phase of creative cycle, undergoes involution in the lowest orders of world manifestation out of His own Free Will, and again, He evolves in gradual steps to reach the apex of the creative cycle to become divine, which He always is. These two phases of His existence in which He alternates as universe are technically called *unmeṣa* (lit. opening out) and *nimeṣa* (lit. closing up). This is the position looking from the point of view of the Supreme Lord.

Looking however from the angle of the individual being in the world, who is fettered (*baddha*) and also covered by various kinds of defilements such as *āṇavamala*, *mayīyamala* and *kārmamala*, and therefore bereft of divine Powers such as omniscience, omnipotence, omnipresence, etc, and also oblivious of his divine nature, the position is somewhat different. The fettered being, technically called *paśu*, has to awake, arise and follow a particular mode of discipline in order to regain his divine Nature. He 'awakes' from 'slumber' only after the influx of Divine Grace on him, the amount of which, as we have already observed, is dependent on his capacity to receive it. Thereafter he arises and follows the path of discipline as directed by the *guru* to remove completely the traces of the *mayīya* and *kārma malas* so that his divine Essence, which has been lying dormant, may become manifest in him.

The starting point in the spiritual journey to the ultimate End differs from individual to individual because of the differentiation in the intensity of divine Grace received by them from the highest Source. We have already discussed the possible reasons for the same. The *Tantras* believe that every individual has to devise his own mode of spiritual discipline or *sādhanā*, keeping in view his needs and inclinations (which have been indicated in the chapter *Dīkṣā*). So, theoretically speaking, no two individuals can adopt exactly the same mode of *sādhanā*. It is true that the Śaiva Tantras prescribe three distinct modes of *sādhanā* for all aspirants, who have been broadly classified under three categories from the point of view of the divine grace received by them in most intense, intense and mild forms. But at the same time, it has been categorically stated that generalisation in the field of *sādhanā* is not possible in view of the varying capacity of the individuals and their inclinations, which have to be taken into account while determining the path of spiritual journey which an individual would have to follow. This is the basic feature of the Tantric view of *sādhanā*, which is quite different from that advocated by the various orthodox schools of Indian philosophy. As has already been pointed out, the *Tantras* therefore attach great importance to the *guru*, who not only initiates the individual aspirants and serves as the medium of divine grace, but also supervises directly or indirectly their progress in the spiritual path. The *Tantras* only lay down certain patterns of spiritual discipline from which the individual aspirant choses his own mode, in conformity with their inclinations and needs, under the guidance of a *guru*.

As we have said at the very outset, though the paths to be followed by the individual aspirants differ from person to person, all of them ultimately lead to the attainment of liberation on one hand and perfect union (*samāveśa*) with the Supreme Lord on the other. It is pertinent to point out here that the attainment of liberation in the Tantric view is not the supreme goal of human life, for liberation is a negative concept. Vācaspati Miśra, in his commentary *Sāṁkhya Tattva Kaumudī* on the *Sāṁkhya Kārikā* of Īśvara Kṛṣṇa has rightly pointed out that liberation means absence of bondage, which is due to ignorance. The attainment of discriminative wisdom (*viveka jñāna*) results in the destruction of ignorance, which, in turn, puts an end to the bondage, thus the attainment of liberation. This view is also supported by the Advaita Vedāntins of the Śaṅkara School. The *Tantras* consider liberation to be a 'smaller ideal' compared to the attainment of one's divinity, which implies and includes the manifestation of the divine Glory in the individual being. It is of course achieved as soon as the individual *sādhaka* receives the divine Grace from the highest Source. For, as we have already observed, it is said that the influx of divine grace in the individual *sādhaka* puts an end to the self-imposed limitation (*nigraha or ātma saṅkoca*). As a result of this, the individual no longer remains a fettered being (*pāsa baddha paśu*). He attains *Śivatva* almost instantaneously as it were, though he is not able to enjoy the fruits of his achievement in the form of divine powers, which remain hidden under the sheaths of *kārma* and *māyīya malas*. To remove these sheaths, he has to make personal efforts in the form of spiritual discipline or *sādhanā* as laid down under different *upāyas* or ways of spiritual discipline. When he succeeds in eradicating completely the two *malas* mentioned above through his intense personal endeavour, he 'recognises' his divine nature and enjoys the fruits of his divinity. The attainment of *Śivatva* is the Supreme Goal of life, the ultimate Destiny. When a *sādhaka* achieves this, the universe around him does not melt away or disappear from his view, he continues to experience the same as an "expression of His Divine Glory", a sport (*sarvam mamaiva vibhavaḥ*). A new meaning is imparted to the universe around him, which appears to him only as His self-expansion. He thus not only achieves the divine status for himself, but divinises every phase of manifestation around him. He no longer remains a *paśu* but raises himself to the state of *Paśupati*. This is the *summum bonum*, the journey's End. Thus the *Tantras* do not 'negate' but rather 'integrate', which has been beautifully described by the well-known Vedic mantra *purṇamidaṁ pūrṇamada* etc. His existence does not come to an end immediately, but he realises his fuller nature, his bliss nature till the physical body falls off.

Between the *summum bonum* and the achievement of liberation following the influx of divine Grace lie the various states of divine enjoyment (*bhoga*), which a particular aspirant can aspire for and enjoy, such as the status of *ādhikārika devatās* (presiding Deities) of different regions, etc, which have already been referred to in the chapter on *Dīkṣā*.

Select Bibliography

Original Sanskrit Texts

Agitāgama, ed. N.R. Bhatt, Pondicherry.

Ānandalaharī, (Śaṅkārācarya), ed. with the commentaries of Rāghavabhaṭṭa, Bhāskararāya and Lakṣmīdhara, Bombay.

Āgama Sāra, ed. P. Shastri, Navabharata Publishers, Calcutta.

Īśvara Pratyabhijña Vimarśinī, ed. by Mukundaram Shastri, Vols. I-II, Srinagar, 1918 *et seq.*

Karpūrādi Stotra, ed. A. Avalon, Ganesh & Co., Madras.

Kāmakalā Vilāsa, ed. A. Avalon, Ganesh & Co., Madras.

Kāmākhyā Tantra, ed. P. Shastri, Navabharat Publishers, Calcutta.

Kālīvilāsa Tantra, ed. P.C. Tarkatirtha, Madras.

Kulārṇava Tantra, ed. Taranath Vidyarnava and A. Avalon, Motilal Banarsidass, Varanasi, 1975.

Kulacūḍāmaṇi Tantra, Sampurnanand Sanskrit University, Varanasi.

Gandharva Tantra, Pub. Kashmir Series of Texts and Studies, Srinagar.

Tantrāloka, (Abhinavagupta), ed. with Comm. of Jayaratha and Śivopādhyāya by Mukundarama Sastri, Vol. I-XII, Srinagar, 1918 *et seq*.

Tantra Sāra, (Abhinavagupta), ed. Mukundaram Shastri, Srinagar, 1918.

Tantrābhidhāna, ed. A. Avalon, Madras.

Tantrarāja Tantra, ed. A. Avalon, Madras.

Tantra Saṁgraha, ed. R.P. Tripathi, Vol. I-IV, Sampurnanand Sanskrit University, Varanasi.

Tārābhakti Sudhārṇava, Pub. Sampurnanand Sanskrit Univ., Varanasi.

Toḍala Tantra, ed. P. Shastri, Navabharat Publishers, Calcutta.

Tripurārahasya, Tātparyadīpikā ṭīkā, ed. Gopinath Kaviraj, Sampurnanand Sanskrit Univ., Varanasi.

Nitya Soḍiskārṇava, ed. with Ṛjuvimarśini ṭīka by B.B. Dvivedi, Varanasi.

Niruttara Tantra, ed. P. Shastri, Navabharat Publishers, Calcutta.

Netra Tantra, ed. with the comm. of Kṣemarāja, Vol. I and II, Srinagar.

Paramārtha Sāra, (Abhinavagupta), ed. J.C. Chatterji, Srinagar, 1916.

Parā Tantra, Pub. Sampurnananda Sanskrit Univ., Varanasi.

Paramānanta Tantra, ed. R.N. Misra, Varanasi.

Parātriṁśika with *Vivaraṇa*, comm. of Abhinavagupta, ed. Mukundaram Shastri, Srinagar, 1918.

Pratyabhijñahṛdaya, (Kṣemarāja), ed. J.C. Chatterji, Srinagar, 1911.

Pheṭakāriṇī Tantra, ed. P. Shastri, Navabharat Publishers, Calcutta.

Bhāskarī, (Bhāskara), ed. K.C. Pandey and K.A.S. Iyer, Vl. I-II, Allahabad.

Bhūtaḍāmara Tantra, ed. P. Shastri, Navabharat Publishers, Calcutta.

Mahānirvāṇa Tantra, with comm. by Hariharanandabharati, ed. Jivananda, Calcutta, 1884.

Mahārtha Mañjarī, ed. B.B. Dvivedi, Varanasi.

Mantramahodadhi, Navabharata Publishers, Calcutta.

Mālinīvijayottara Tantra, ed. Madhusadana Kaul, Srinagar, 1922.

Mālinīvijaya Vārtika, (Abhinavagupta), ed. Madhusudana Kaul, Srinagar, 1921.

Mṛgendra Tantra, ed. with comm. of Rāma Kaṇṭha, Srinagar.

Mṛgendra Tantra, ed. N.R. Bhatt, Pondicherry.

Yoginīhṛdaya, ed. G.N. Kaviraj, Sarasvati Bhavan, Varanasi.

Rudrayāmala Tantra, ed. B.P. Tripathi, Sampurnananda Sanskrit Univ., Varanasi, 1980.

Rauravāgama, ed. N.R. Bhatt, Pondicherry.

Vijñānabhairava Tantra, ed. Mukundarama Shastri, Srinagar, 1918.

Vāma Keśvarīmata, ed. with comm. by Jayaratha, Srinagar.

Sarvollāsa Tantra, (Kṛṣṇānanda Āgamavagiśa), Navabharata Publishers, Calcutta.

Svacchanda Tantra, ed. with comm. of Kṣemarāja by Madhusudan Kaul Vol. I-VI Srinagar, 1921 *et seq*.

Spanda Kārikā, ed. with *Vṛtti* of Kallaṭa by J.C. Chatterji, Srinagar, 1916.

Spanda Nirṇaya, (Kṣemarāja), ed. Madhusudana Kaul, Srinagar, 1925.

Spanda Sandoha, (Kṣemarāja), ed. Mukundarama Shastri, Srinagar, 1917.

Śāradā Tilaka.

Śiva Sūtra with *Vimarśini* comm. of Kṣemarāja, ed. J.C. Chatterji, Srinagar 1911.

Śiva Dṛṣti, (Somānanda), ed. Madusudan Kaul Srinagar, 1924.

Śrīvidyārṇava Tantra, ed. with comm. by Vidyāraṇya, Srinagar.

Saṣcaktniruparṇa, ed. A. Avalon, Madras.

Sattriṁśatattva Sandoha, (Ananda Kavi), ed. D.B. Sen Sharma, Kurukshetra, 1977.

General Books

Avalon, A., *The Tantra of Great Liberation*, Madras.

Bagche, P.C., *Studies in the Tantras*, Vol. I-II Calcutta, 1939.

Bhandarkar, R.G., *Vaisnavism, Saivism and Minor Religious Systems*, Poona, 1928.

Chakravarti, C., *Tantra Paricaya*, Visvabharat, Calcutta.

Das Gupta, S.N., *A History of Indian Philosophy*, Vol. V, Cambridge, 1962.

Goudriaan, T., *Hindu Tantrik and Sakta Literature*, Utrecht, 1980.

Farquhar, J.N., *An Outline of the Religious Literature in India*, London, 1920.

Kaviraj, G.N., *Bhāratīya Saṁskṛti Aur Sādhanā*, Vol. I-II (in Hindi), Patna, 1957.

——, *Bhāratīya Sādhanār Dhārā* (in Bengali), Calcutta, 1955.

——, *Tāntrika Sādhanā O' Siddhānta* (in Bengali), Vol. I, Burdwan.

——, *Tantra O Āgama Śastre Digdarśaṇa* (in Bengali) Vol. I, Calcutta. 1963.

——, *Tāntrika Vāṅgmaya meṅ Śākta Dṛṣṭi* (in Hindi), Patna, 1965.

——, *Tāntrika Sāhitya*, Varanasi.

——, 'Śākta Philosophy', a chapter in *The Philosophy of East and West*, ed. by S. Radhakrishnan, London, 1951.

Mehta, P.D., *Early Indian Religious Thought*, London, 1956.

Pandeya, K.C., *Abhinavagupta, An Historical and Philosophical Study*, Chowkhamba, 1929.

Sinha, J.N., *History of Indian Philosophy*, Vol. II, Calcutta.

Woodroffe, J., *Principles of Tantra*, Vol. I-II, Madras.

——, *Garland of Letters*, Madras.

——, *Śakti and Śākta*, Madras.

——, *Mahāmāyā*, Madras.

——, *Serpent Power*, Madras.

Glossary

ābhāsa	Self-manifestation
adhva	Order or Level of manifestation in creation
aham	Self experience as pure 'I'
aiśvarya	Divine Glory
āmarśa	Self experience
ānanda śakti	Divine Śakti in the aspect of Delight
āṇavamala	Defilement in the form of self-contraction
anugraha	Divine Grace
anuttara	The Absolute
bauddha ajñāna	Intellectual ignorance
bauddha jñāna	Spiritual knowledge on the intellectual level
bindu	Divine Śakti in a potential form
cidaṇu	Spirit in the form of monadic Pure Consciousness
cit śakti	Divine Śakti in the form of Pure Illumination
citi	Pure Illumination of Consciousness
dīkṣā	Initiation
guru	Spiritual teacher who acts as the medium for the transmission of Divine Grace
icchā	Divine will
icchā śakti	Divine śakti in the aspect of Divine Will
idam	Universe symbolised as the Pure Object on the Pure Order
indriya	Sense organ
kalā	An aspect of Divine Śakti; one of the five *kañcukas* causing limited authorship

kāla	Time; one of the five *kañcukas* causing confinement of the individual soul to time
kañcuka	Sheath for self-concealment
kārma mala	Defilement in the form of residual impressions of past deeds.
kriyā śakti	Divine Śakti in the aspect of action
Mahāmāyā	Divine Power operating on the level of Pure Order
mala	Defilement
maṇḍala	Construction of cosmic symbols
māyīya mala	Defilement caused by Māyā and its five *kañcukas*
mudrā	Making proper gestures
nigraha	Self-limitation
nimeṣa	Closing up
nyāsa	Assignment of powerful sounds or symbols on the body
Parama Śiva	Supreme Śiva who is the Supreme Reality
parāmarśa	Self-experience
Parameśvara	Supreme Lord
parapramātā	Supreme Experiencer
pāṣa	Fetter or bond
paśu	Fethered being
paśu pramātā	Limited-experiencer
pauruṣa ajñāna	Spiritual Knowledge consequent on the destruction of self-limitation
prakāśa	Pure Illumination
pralaya	Cosmic dissolution
pralayākala	A type of disembodied soul
pūrṇāhamtā	Supreme self-experience as the pure 'I' on the highest level

pūrṇatva	Fullness
rāga	One of the five sheaths causing the development of attachment in the spiritual monad (*cidaṇu*)
sakala	Embodied soul
śaktipāta	Descent of divine grace
saṁskāra	Residual impression
Saṁvid	Supreme experiencing principle
saṅkalpa	Divine resolve
saṅkoca	Self-contraction
śivatva	Highest state of realisation; Self-experience as Śiva
śuddha vikalpa	Pure experience, experience of the Self in the pure self on the intellectual plane
śunya	Cosmic void
tattva	A level of creation
unmeṣa	Opening out
upāya	Way of self-realisation
vāk	Logos; Primordial Word
varṇa	Letter; letter symbolising different aspects of Divine Śakti
varṇamāla	Garland of letters
vijñānākala	Divine power; the Supreme Lord in His dynamic aspect
vikalpa	Concept
vimarśa	Pure Consciousness in the aspect of dynamism

Index

The words are arranged in the order of the English alphabet; Sanskrit technical terms are given in italics.

Abhinavagupta 19, 41, 87, 95, 138, 141
ādhāra (locus) 141
Āgamas 18
—, seven salient features of the 18
Aham 72
ājñācakra 141
Ambā 45
anāhata nāda 146
ānanda 54, 65
— *śakti* 65
āṇavamala 71, 74, 147
—, two kinds of 74
āṇavapāya 129
aṇḍaja 79
anubhavavākya 124
anugraha 67
— or *śaktipāta* 90, 92
anupāyadīkṣā 104
apāna 135
Asaṅga 21
aśuddha adhva (impure realm) 68
Aśvakrāntā 22
Atharvaveda 13
Aurobindo, Sri 80
Bagalā 47
Bagchi, P.C. 21
Bahurūpaṣṭaka Tantras 31
bauddha ajñāna or intellectual ignorance 79, 84, 86
Bhadra Kālī 42
Bhairava 33, 131
Bhairava Tantra 32, 130
Bhairavāṣṭaka Tantras 29
Bhairavī 46
Bharga Śikhā Tantra 32
Bhaṭṭa 33
bhoga deha 78
Bhrāmarī 45
Bhuvaneśvarī 46
bījamantras 125
— originated from *sañjalpa* 125
bodies, two kinds of 79
body, determination of the type of 78
body-apparatus, different kinds of 78
Brahman 63, 64
Brāhmaṇa texts 121
cakras 142
Candrajñāna 41
Chinnamastā 47
cidaṇus, two distinct types 74
cit śakti 65
daiva śarira 78
Dakṣiṇa Kālī 42
dakṣinācāra 49
Dakṣiṇāmnāya 24
defilements (*malas*) 71
deśa (space) 141
dhāraṇās 130, 131
Dhūmāvatī 47
dīkṣā (initiation) 103, 108

—, *āṇavī* 104, 105
—, *āṇavī*, ten kinds of 106
—, *jñāna* 116
—, kinds of 104
—, *kriyā* 116
—, *lokadharmiṇī* 107, 113
—, *nirbīja* 107
—, *putraka* 107, 111
—, *sabīja* 107, 114
—, *sadyonirvāṇadāyinī* 114
—, *śakti* 104, 105
—, *sāmayī* 108, 111
—, *śāmbhavī* 104
—, *śivadharminī* 107, 112
divine freedom (*ahetukī kṛpā*), unconditional act of 95
Divine Nature (*Śivatva*) 147
dvadaśānta 144
eight-limbed (*aṣṭānga*) ethico-psychological discipline 83
Ekayana Śākhā of Śukla Yajurveda 23
Eliade, Mircea 53
equilibrium between liberation and enjoyment 87
evolution (*aroha*) 80
first step: purgation 82
five faces of Lord Śiva 24, 52
five kinds of intuitive experience 54
five *mahābhūtas* 79
five '*makāras*' 56
five principal heads 65
five principles of limitation (*kañcukas*) 75
five-fold *prāṇa vāyu* 135
four types of *sadgurus* 98
four kinds of gross physical body 79
four kinds of *yogins* 101
ghūrṇi 54
grace, characteristic signs of divine 93
grace, nine kinds of divine 92
gross physical body 79
Guhyabheda 36
Gūhyeśvarī 45
Guru (divine teacher) 96
guru, akalpita 98
—, *akalpitakālpaka* 98, 99
—, *asad* (not-real teacher) 98
—, *daiva* 100
—, *kula* 98
—, *puruṣa* 100, 101
—, *siddha* 100
—, two types of 94
—, *vidyā* 98
Hādividyā 45
hamsa, representing *so 'ham* 123
Hevajra Tantra 21
Hṛdbheda Tantra 36
icchā 65
— *śakti* 66
iḍā 141
ignorance, two distinct kinds of 84
impure realm 68
Indian Philosophy 127, 134
initiation: see *dīkṣā*
Īśāna 28
Īśvara tattva 72
Jangama Raudra 33
jarāyuja 79
jīvanmukti 86, 87
jñāṇa 65
— *dīkṣā* 107
— *śakti* 66
jñānendriyas 143
Kādividyā 45
Kahādividyā 45
Kalasaṁkirśaṇī Kālī 42
kāla (time) 76, 141

kalā 75
Kāla Kālī 42
Kālāmukhas 33
Kālānala 33
Kālī 42, 43
Kalpasūtra of Paraśurāma 22
kalpita guru 98, 99
kalpitakalpaka guru 100
kalpitākalpita guru 98
Kāma Kālī 42
Kāmākṣī 45
Kamalā 47
Kāmika 36
Kāmikāgama 17, 28
kampa 54, 55
kañcukas 76
Kāpālikas 33
karmabījas 77
karma-deha 78
karmamala 77, 147
kārmic seeds 77
Kāruṇika Saiva 33
Kaula School 48
Kaviraj, G.N. 14, 15, 21, 33, 34, 42, 144
knowledge, path of 128
Krama School 33, 34
Krama Vallī 34
Kramastotra and *Kramkeli* 34
Kramasūkta 34
kriyā 65
— *dikṣā* 107
— *śakti* 66
kriyopāya 130
Kṣapaṇaka 33
Kuṇḍalini śakti 49, 145
— lying coiled up at the *mūlādhāra cakra* 97
Kubjikā 42
Kubjikā Tantras 36
Kumārī 45
Lakṣmīdhara 34, 35, 37
Lakuliśapāśupata 32
liberation as absence of bondage 149
madhyamā 19, 24, 122
madhyanāḍī (middle channel) 141, 142
Mahābhārata 17
Mahādeva Tantra 36
Mahālakṣmī 45
Mahāmāyā 68
Mahārthamañjarī 34
Mahārthodaya 34
mahāvākyas 123
Mahāvidyās, ten 41
Mahāvratins 33
Maitreyanātha 21
malas 71
—, maturation of (*mala paripāka*) 94
makāras 50
—, hidden meaning of 51, 56
—, literal meaning of 56
Mālinīvidyā 36
Maṅgalacandī 45
mantra (sacred word) 118, 119
— as consciousness-light (*cinmarīcayaḥ*) 119
—, 'implant' in seed form 118
— in *sādhanā* 123
—, seers of 120
mantradraṣṭā 120
mantras, Vedic 20, 121
mānuṣa śarīra 78
Mātaṅgī 47
Māyā śakti 65, 68, 75, 135
mayīyamala 75, 147
Mukundabali 34
nāḍīs 57, 141, 142, 145

Nāgārjuna 21
Nandikeśvara Saiva 32
Nandīśikhā Tantra 32
nidrā 54, 55
Nigraha 67
Nitya Tantra 32
obscuration (*tirodhānakarī*), universal power of 75
Pādukodaya 34
pañca kṛtyā kārī (doer of five functions) 67
pañca-makāra sādhanā 50
Pāñcarātra Āgamas 23
Pandey, K.C. 32
parā 122
Parāsaṁvid 60, 140
—, supreme Experiencing Principle 60
—, two-fold nature of 60
Parāstotra 34
Parāvāk 19
Paścimāmnāya 24
paśu pramātā 73
Pāśupata 32
paśyantī 19, 24, 122
Patañjali 13
pauruṣa ajñāna 72, 84, 85
piṇḍasiddhi 112
piṅgalā 141
Prabodha Candrodaya 33
Pradīpikā 142
Prakṛti śakti 69
prāṇa 132-135
— *śakti* 136, 137, 141, 143
— *vāyu* 134, 135
prāṇamaya kośa 135
prāṇoccāra 141, 144
prārabdha karma 87
prātibhijñāna 99
pure object (*idam*) 72
pure realm 68
Pūrṇeśvarī 42
Pūrvamnāya 24
rāga 76
Rāmakṛṣṇa 42
Rāmaprasāda 42
Raseśvara Saiva 32
Rathakrāntā 22
Raudrāgamas 25, 27, 28
recognition of one's Śiva-nature (*Śivatva*) 59
Rudra Tantra 32
Sadāśiva tattva 72
sadguru (real divine teacher) 98
sādhakas 113
—, *śivadharmiṇī* and *lokadharmiṇī* 112
Sadyojāta 28
Sahajīyā Buddhists 88
Śaiva schools, eight 32
Śaiva schools, thirteen 33
Śaiva Siddhānta 32
Śaiva Tantras 25
Śaivāgamas 25
Śakti, divine 61
Śakti (*spanda*) 143
śaktipāta 83, 89, 90
Śāktopāya 129
Śāmbhavopāya 129
samāna 135
saṁhāra 67
sampuṭita ('encased form') 125
Saṁvid or *caitanya* (pure consciousness) 136, 137, 139
Saṁvidullāsa 34
Saundaryalahirī 34, 35, 37
self-expansion of Parama Śiva 61
self-manifestation of Śiva as the universe 61

Siddha Tantra 32
Śikhaṣṭaka Tantras 31
Śivatva 91, 147
Śmaśāna Kālī 42
Ṣoḍaśī 44
Somasiddhāntins 33
Śrīkaṇṭhī Saṁhitā 26
Śrīvidyā 42, 44
sthiti 67
subtle body 79
śuddha adhva 68
Sundarī 45
svātantrya śakti 61
svedaja 79
tantra, etymology of 17
Tantras, the 64 37
—, twenty-four marks of 18
Tantrabheda 36
Tantrāloka 19, 25, 41, 95, 141
Tantrasāra 87, 95, 116, 141
Tārā 44
Tatpuruṣa 28
tiryag-śarīra 78
Todala Tantra 37
Todalottara Tantra 36
trāṇatā 119
Trika Śaiva 32
Tripurasundarī 44
triveṇī 141
twilight language (*saṁdhyā bhāṣā*) 53
udāna 135
udbhava 54
udbhija 79
Underhill 53
universe as expression of Divine Glory 149
unmeṣa (opening out) 62, 139, 147
— and *nimeṣa* 62
Upaniṣads 63, 64, 132
upāyas: *icchopāya*, *jñānopāya* and *kriyopāya* 129
Ūrdhvāmnāya 25
Uttarāmnāya 24
Vācaspati Miśra 33
Vāgīśāṣṭaka Tantras 31
vaikharī 19, 24, 122
— *varṇa* 119
Vaikhānasa School 24
Vaikhānasa Āgamas 23
Vaiṣṇava Tantras 23
vāk 121, 122
Vāmā Kālī 42
vāmācāra 49
Vāmadeva 28
vāmajuṣṭa 36
Vāmaka 33
Vāmakeśvara Tantra 34
Vārāhī Tantra *18*
Vātula 36
Vātulottara 36
Vedic seers, experiences of 121
vidyā 75
Vijñāna Bhairava 130, 131
vijñānākalas 74
Vindhyavāsinī 45
Vīraśaiva 32
Viśālakṣī 45
Viśiṣṭādvaita Śaiva of Śrīkaṇṭha 32
Viṣṇukrāntā 22
Viśveśvarī 42
vyāna 135
Yāmalas 18
Yāmalas, eight distinguishing characteristics 18
Yāmalāṣṭaka Tantras 29
Yāmunācārya 33
Yoga Sūtra 83, 85, 135

Other books of related interest
published by **Indica Books**:

- **Abhinavagupta's Commentary on the Bhagavad Gita**
  Gītārtha Saṁgraha
  English Transl. by Boris Marjanovic
- **The Aphorisms of Shiva**
  The Śiva Sūtra with Bhāskara's Commentary, the Vārttika
  Transl. by Mark S.G. Dyczkowski
- **The Stanzas of Vibration**
  The Spandakārikā with Four Commentaries
  Transl. by Mark S.G. Dyczkowski
- **A Journey in the World of the Tantras**
  by Mark S.G. Dyczkowski
- **Vijnana Bhairava : The Practice of Centring Awareness**
  Sanskrit text, English translation and Commentary by
  Swami Lakshman Joo
- **Shaivism: A Study of the Agamic, Epic and Puranic Periods**
  by N.R. Bhatt
- **The Hindu Pantheon in Nepalese Line Drawings**
  Two Manuscripts of the Pratiṣṭhālakṣaṇasārasamuccaya
  Compiled by Gudrun Bühnemann
- **स्पन्दप्रदीपिका** *Spandapradīpikā* (Sanskrit)
  A Commentary on the Spandakārikā by Bhagavadutpalācārya
  Edited by Mark S.G. Dyczkowski
- **Exposition of Reasoning**
  Tarkabhāṣā
  Transl. by M.M. Pt. Ganganath Jha
- **Selected Writings of M.M. Gopinath Kaviraj**
- **The Book of Aghor Wisdom**
  by Baba Bhagwan Ram